CHRISTIANS IN THE WARSAW GHETTO

Christians in the Warsaw Ghetto

An Epitaph for the Unremembered

Peter F. Dembowski

University of Notre Dame Press

Notre Dame, Indiana

Manufactured in the United States of America

Library of Congress Cataloging-in-Publication Data

Dembowski, Peter F. (Peter Florian), 1925–
Christians in the Warsaw ghetto : an epitaph for the unremembered /
by Peter F. Dembowski.
p.   cm.
Includes bibliographical references and index.
ISBN 0-268-02572-X (hardcover : alk. paper)
ISBN 0-268-02573-8 (pbk. : alk. paper)
1. Jewish Christians—Poland—Warsaw.
2. Warsaw (Poland)—Church history.   I. Title.
BR158.D46   2005
940.53'1853841—dc22

2005019660

∞ *This book is printed on acid-free paper.*

Dedicated to the sacred memory of

Janina Landy Dembowska,

ma plus que mère

CONTENTS

ACKNOWLEDGMENTS

Many people encouraged me in the writing of this book. My gratitude goes to Alina Brodzka Wald of Warsaw and M. Louis-Christophe Zaleski-Zamenhof of Paris, both former children of the Warsaw ghetto, for having shared their memories with me. I thank my Canadian summer neighbors, Elisabeth Gauthier, Yvon Gauthier, Pierre Martel, and Claude Bruneau, the first readers of a very rough draft. I wish to express my gratitude to my friends and colleagues at the University of Chicago: the late Howard Moltz, professor of biopsychology; Ralph Lerner, professor in the Committee on Social Thought; Martin Marty, Bernard McGinn, and David Tracy, professors in the Divinity School; as well as to Barry Sullivan, attorney-at-law and an early and perspicacious reader of my manuscript. David Bade, monographic cataloguer extraordinaire at the University of Chicago Library, was the first person to struggle with the rough draft and weed out the numerous Polonisms and Gallicisms from my text. His assistance in tracking down difficult-to-find Yiddish and Polish documents was invaluable. I also thank my former student Steven Feldman, the managing director of *Biblical Archeology Review,* for his suggestions. I wish to express my debt to Havi Ben-Sasson of the Yad Vashem Institute in Jerusalem for cheerfully and rapidly supplying me with the documents I sought. During my trip to Warsaw in March 2001, I profited greatly from conversations with Rev. Zdzisław Król and Rev. Tadeusz Karolak, the present-day pastors of, respectively, the Church of the Nativity of the Blessed Virgin Mary and the Church of All Saints. Their knowledge and keen historical sense were of inestimable assistance to me. Monsignor Tadeusz Uszyński of the Saint Andrew Church in Warsaw, a proud bearer of Israel's "Righteous among the Nations" award and very knowledgeable about the history of the Warsaw ghetto, guided my research in Warsaw by introducing me to important sources. I wish to thank my Polish colleague Sławomir Łukasiewicz of the Catholic University of Lublin for supplying me with the basic bibliography of the subject and for offering me helpful bibliographical advice. I thank also Jacek Leociak of the University of Warsaw for letting me read the then still unpublished part of his book on the Warsaw ghetto and for sharing with me his vast knowledge of the subject. I am grateful to the director of the Jewish Historical Institute in Warsaw, Feliks Tych, for granting me an interview and, above all, to Ruta Sakowska, who was good enough to talk to me at length about my project, despite the precarious state of her health. I wish to thank my nephew, Piotr Rodowicz, for taking care of me in Warsaw and for supplying me with many precious details from the pen of his father, Władysław Rodowicz, historian of the family. My thanks go to my brother, Monsignor Bronisław Dembowski, bishop of Włocławek in Poland, with whom I shared the memories of the events taking place between 1939 and 1944 in Poland. He checked the veracity of our memories and has always encouraged me to undertake and to complete this work. Finally, I owe a debt of gratitude to the University of Notre Dame Press and its director, Barbara Hanrahan, and, above all, to Rabbi Michael Signer of the Theology Department of that university for his careful assessment of my manuscript and for his priceless suggestions concerning some of my initial assumptions.

The University of Chicago,
January 2004

CHRISTIANS IN THE WARSAW GHETTO

INTRODUCTION

Ever since the 1970s the Holocaust—as the destruction of European Jewry began to be generally called at that time—has been the subject of an ongoing historical, philosophical, and theological debate centered on one basic question. Was the Holocaust a unique historical event, or was it rather an example, albeit the most extreme one, among the other genocides that have occurred? The debate is far from being settled and will doubtless erupt again, for it is not a distinction of slight importance whether, for instance, the destruction of Armenians in 1915, the vast manmade starvation in Ukraine in 1936–37, or the mass killing in Cambodia in 1975–79 should be spoken of as "holocausts" in their own rights.

Although it is not the purpose of the present work to resolve what is, I believe, an irresolvable issue, I am not neutral on the issue. I believe that this work shows—from a usually forgotten vantage point—that the Holocaust of European Jews was a catastrophe unique in history. It was unique in the long history of anti-Jewish activities because it involved the radical redefinition of the victimized group by the victimizer.

———

I am fully conscious of the fact that most Jews view conversion from Judaism to Christianity with apprehension. I am also aware that Jews' and Christians' divergent views on conversion constitute one of the most contentious aspects of the relations between them. In examining the attitudes of most ghetto dweller toward their fellow sufferers—Christians of Jewish origin—we must bear in mind that Jewish attitudes toward conversion are an integral part of traditional attitudes formed by age-long historical experience and thinking.

In the very long history of Jewish-Christian relations—a history which began with the conversion from Judaism of the first Christians—the prevailing rabbinic opinion has always maintained that Jewishness is an inalienable

1

status of all the "descendants of Abraham."[1] Thus Jewish attitudes toward converts stem from a Jew's very concept of what is to be a Jew. Failing to grasp the gist of this concept would surely lead us to misunderstand those Jews who wrote about Christians living in the Warsaw ghetto.

Perhaps the best way for a non-Jew to understand the Jewish view of Jewishness, and consequently Jewish attitudes to converts, is to cite a recent work by Michael Wyschogrod, a Jewish philosopher quite familiar with Christianity. The very title of his book: *The Body of Faith: God in the People Israel,* takes one a long way toward understanding the Jewish concept of Jewishness. In his chapter "A Chosen Nation," Wyschogrod attempts a definition of Jewish philosophy, and Jewish philosophers, and by extension his views define any Jew. Discussing Jewish aspects in the philosophies of both Marx and Freud, he states:

> Yet the fact remains that Marx and Freud are considered Jews irrespective of their opinions. This would not be so of someone born Christian who declared himself an atheist. It would not occur to anyone to refer to such a person as a Christian philosopher. It would therefore seem that being Jewish is significantly different than being Christian. Christianity is a set of beliefs as reflected in conduct. No one can be a Christian and explicitly deny the basic tenets of Christianity. . . . [W]hether verified verbally or by conduct, being Christian is incompatible with the holding of some beliefs. A Jew whose conduct violates the teaching of Judaism or one who verbally denies fundamental Jewish beliefs remains a Jew, though not a very good one. (1989, 42–43)

Later in the book, Wyschogrod sums up the the fundamental distinction between the self-definitions of Jewish and Christian communities, definitions rooted in religious concepts:

> While the Church also sees itself as a community, it is a community of believers that it understands itself. The bonds among Christians are therefore not family bonds. But Judaism's teaching is that it is the election of a human family—the seed of Abraham—that es-

---

1. For the early Jewish history of the controversy concerning the "Jewish status" of converts to Christianity, see Katz (1961, 67–81). Katz discusses Jewish-Gentile relations from the time of the early rabbinic Judaism until the second half of the nineteenth century.

tablishes a family of election through which salvation comes to humanity. . . . The bond that unites Jews is not an idea and remains operative whether or not there is ideological agreement. (254)

It is obvious that this Jewish concept of Jewishness and the Christian concept of what it is to be Christian are diametrically opposed. For most Christians, a baptized person has always been considered Christian, unless the sincerity of conversion was seriously questioned. It is perhaps ironic that many anti-Semites who are nominally Christians do question Jewish converts' sincerity and agree with the largely held Jewish opinion that converts are motivated by self-interest and materialistic gain rather than religious reasons.

Many Christians agree with Wyschogrod and understand the way in which Marx and Freud remained Jews. The former was the son of a German Jew who had nominally become a Protestant in order to be admitted to the legal profession, and the latter never converted. What many Christians find more difficult to understand is that by embracing Christianity a Jew cut his relation with Judaism in a more radical way than if he embraced, for example, the militantly atheistic Marxism. There are, of course, serious theological and historical reasons for this, since embracing Christianity precludes the very acceptance of the Jewish concept of Jewish community, whereas becoming a communist simply implies an ideological disagreement with Judaism.

In order to understand and appreciate the opinions concerning the Christianized Jews held by Jewish ghetto dwellers like Emanuel Ringelblum, the archivist and the chief organizer of the intellectual resistance in the ghetto, as well as the opinions of Christians in the ghetto or outside it, we have to accept the incompatibility of Jewish and Christian views of their respective communities and, at the same time, understand both views. In other words, both Jews and Christians should clearly understand on what they agree, on what they disagree, and on what they agree to disagree. Without this commitment, many Jewish or Christian opinions cited in this work may well appear strange or odd.

In the specific Polish situation of the period before World War II, in practical everyday life the difference between the nationalistic way one defined "Jewishness" and the way one defined "Polishness" was far less striking than historical, philosophical, and theological attitudes might have implied. Seen in the cultural situation of Jewish and Polish society, the difference between the theological definitions of "national" Judaism (*Knesses Israel*) and of a Christian community of believers became less than obvious. National feeling took over. For several generations, religion served, in fact, largely as a simplified "national" identifier: a Christian Orthodox was a Russian, a Protestant was a German, a Uniate Catholic was a Ukrainian, a Roman Catholic was a Pole, and a Jew was, naturally, a Jew. Since the nineteenth century, the steady growth of nationalism accentuated this popular mode of thinking. To take but one example, the identification of Catholicism with "Polishness" can be clearly seen in the memoirs of the medical scientist Ludwik Hirszfeld, a Christian convert.

There were numerous reasons why an individual living in Poland might convert; doubtless each conversion had its own history. Discussion in depth of the various reasons for conversion lies outside the purview of this study. It is necessary to point out, however, certain specific historical facts concerning Polish Jewry. While there undoubtedly were some Polish Jews who converted to Christianity for reasons other than religious ones, the Jewish situation in Poland was quite different from that which prevailed in Western Europe and, more specifically, in Germany. In the Polish situation, there were far fewer pressures to embrace Christianity, such as those undoubtedly used on the elder Marx. In the nineteenth century and later, when emerging nationalism brought about such pressures, Poles did not have much administrative control in their territories run by Russians and Germans. In Austrian Poland, the situation resembled the general situation prevailing in the Austro-Hungarian Empire, but even there, the comparison with the situation of other European Jews can be misleading.

The subject treated in this book inevitably touches on other important issues. The first is anti-Semitism: the cultural, "visceral," anti-Semitism in prewar Poland; its parallel, the economical anti-Semitism stemming from competition; and the vicissitudes of anti-Semitism during the war. It is impossible in such a work as this to treat this subject in any detail. In the United States, there is the firmly established opinion that Poles were notoriously anti-Semitic, an opinion shared by Jews and non-Jews alike. I share in this opinion, but conscious of my Polish origins, I would like to present an argument for the defense based on historical facts. The reason that in 1939 some 10 percent of the population was Jewish was that they were old refugees from Western Europe and especially from Germany—the land that had given them the language they used in Poland. In the late nineteenth century another wave of Jews came to Poland from Russia. Thus, while accepting the fact of anti-Semitism in Poland, we should bear in mind that, unlike other countries in Europe proud of their lack of anti-Semitism, Poland had historically been a land of asylum for Jews, a land in which they could develop their distinctive culture.

My study touches on other issues also: the attitude of Christians toward baptized Jews, the attitude of the church toward the Jews, and more generally the attitude of any group toward those who leave the group (the "turncoats"). These issues will be dealt with very briefly in my final chapter, along with some comments on the relative paucity of documentation concerning Christian views of baptized Jews.

But the main issue raised by this microhistory is the new definition of a Jew created by the persecutor: the community of Christianized Jews found themselves redefined as Jews and were ordered into the Warsaw ghetto. Unlike the Armenians who had converted to Islam and who were exempt from destruction by the Turks, the Christianized Jews were subject to the same discrimination, persecution, and annihilation as their Jewish kin. Their status as Jews, bestowed on them by the Nazis, had absolutely nothing to do with the Jewish, or for that matter the Christian, considerations of who is and who is not a Jew. They were considered Jews on the grounds of pseudoscientific *race* theory. In bringing this aspect of the Shoah to light, I hope to demonstrate precisely this completely "innovative," "scientific," and "racist" character of Nazi anti-Semitism and thus to underscore the unique character of the Shoah.

I witnessed many of the events described here. I lived in Warsaw during the German occupation of Poland until I left in October 1944. I belong to a generation of the younger participants of World War II, and I remember many things that happened during that calamitous period. I knew many of the Christianized Jews, and I owe a great personal debt to one family of converts who were connected by marriage with my father's family.

While writing this book, I was aware of the shortcomings of one's memory. Having read a great quantity of the memorialist literature concerning the war in Poland, much of it written many years after the events described, I fully appreciate that personal memories can be misleading. But while they can be misleading as to exact facts, dates, and names of persons and places, I believe they are far more reliable in relation to the *atmosphere* of the times. I remember very well the absolute fear and despair, occasional panics, and occasional excesses of hope and joy in the midst of tragic events. And the memory of the *atmosphere* of those terrible times has been reinforced through the years by my dreams, in which the events are often senseless, but the atmosphere is often true.

Thus while I seek to make a microhistorical study, the work is not without its autobiographical component. While I am not a historian of World War II, I was a witness to many things that happened in Warsaw. Had there been studies devoted to the Jewish Christians of Warsaw available in the West, I would not have undertaken my study. I hope that my work will be followed by more fully developed histories of various "minorities" among the victims of the Shoah.

For these reasons I present, in chapter 1, the genesis of my work by offering my reasons, some autobiographical and others historical, for writing about the Jewish converts to Christianity and their descendants who found themselves in the Warsaw ghetto.

In chapter 2, I present certain bibliographical problems that I encountered upon entering the study of baptized Jews. There is, of course, much literature concerning the Shoah in Poland in general and the history of the Warsaw ghetto in particular, but very little has been published specifically on my subject. After having read much of the literature on the Warsaw ghetto, I came to see the need for an explanation of the special circumstances surrounding the provenance, preservation, and diffusion of this literature. The documents I have used were written chiefly in Yiddish and in Polish. In the years immediately following the war, many Yiddish documents were translated into Polish, but it is important to realize that their translation, publication, and dissemination were often prevented or else delayed by the control and censorship of the Communist authorities. Equally important is the self-censorship that invariably resulted from fear of the authoritarian regime. Here again, personal experience cannot be separated from the historian's task. Without understanding this historiographical background, these texts cannot be fully understood. Furthermore, although many important texts are available in good English translations, I was occasionally surprised, to say the least, to find that some of the most important sources are either translated badly or are not available in English at all.

Despite the immense literature concerning the Shoah in general, certain details of the Warsaw ghetto history are not well known outside the circles of specialized historians. Chapter 3 presents a short history of the ghetto which begins with the origin of the "open" quarter, continues through the creation of the closed ghetto and its shrinking, and concludes with the destruction of the greater part of the Warsaw ghetto in July–September 1942, during the "Resettlement," that is, the transport to Treblinka and the liquidation of some 300,000 Warsaw Jews. An appreciation of the basic chronology of the ghetto is necessary for the correct appraisal of certain documents. The gradual worsening of the situation, and the (very) gradual realization of the Nazis' true aims concerning the Jewish population, can be appreciated only with a proper understanding of the passage of time. Thus, a ghetto diarist writing in February 1940 is, in a sense, a different person from the same diarist writing in February 1942, and altogether unlike the one writing in February 1943.

This is a study of the Christianized Jews who were organized in parishes. The Warsaw ghetto was unique in that although there were Christians in other ghettos, only Warsaw had fully functioning parishes.[2] This book would not be complete without an investigation of their participation in the Catholic Church. Therefore, chapter 4 briefly outlines the organization and membership of the three, and later two, Roman Catholic parishes functioning in the Warsaw ghetto until the time of the "Resettlement."

The most important portion of the book consists of a presentation and discussion of Jewish views of the Christians in the ghetto (chap. 5) and the baptized Jews' and and other Christians' views about their situation there (chap. 6). I analyze the contemporary and the postwar writings and comment on them with the aid of hindsight and, it must be said, using my own memories and judgments based on them.

Chapter 7 consists of the conclusions I have drawn from my reading of the sources and my understanding of them. This understanding has doubtless been influenced by my memories and my opinions formed during many years of thinking about the calamitous years of World War II.

———

Most of the documents I consulted in the course of this work are preserved in Polish. If they have not been translated into English, I have provided my own translation. When referring to the titles of untranslated works, I supply, in the bibliography, the original Polish or Yiddish along with the English translation. I also offer the original Polish term or phrase any time it presents a

2. We know, for example, that there were Christians in the second largest ghetto in Poland, in Łódź:

When the ghetto was sealed, numerous Christians also stayed behind. They can be divided into two groups: Those of Jewish origin and Aryans. Although the first were Christians, they were considered Jews and were forced into the ghetto. They were thought of [by other dwellers of the ghetto] as fully Jewish, since they concealed their religion, there being no church services in the ghetto. Although Aryans had the opportunity of leaving, some stayed for various reasons. Many were related to or married to Jews, or, like some maids, were so close to Jewish families that they did not want to abandon them, even in disaster. (Adelson and Lapides 1989, 59–60)

formidable difficulty of translation. For the untranslated Yiddish documents I relied on the assistance of my friend and colleague at the University of Chicago, Elisa Steinberg. I thank her warmly for generously sharing her knowledge and her humor with me.

With the Jewish personal names and family names, I tried to follow as closely as possible the Polish forms that they used, thus Emanuel is written with one *m*, Czerniaków with "closed" *ó*, and so on. However, in the case of common nouns, I followed the English transliteration of the Yiddish terms; for example, *yiddish bukh* (for the Polish transcription *jidisz buch*).[3]

---

3. To facilitate the reading of Polish names and phrases, I offer here a brief note on Polish spelling and promounciation: Polish *c* is always pronounced *ts* (even before *k*); *ch* is *h* (*h*orse); *j* is *y* (as in *y*et); *y* is a back vowel, a little like *i* in b*i*t. *Z* is used in the second part of a consonantal group to indicate the pronunciation of this "double consonant": thus *cz* is *ch* (*ch*urch) or *tch* (tha*tch*); *sz* is *sh* (*sh*ip); *szcz* is *shch* (a*sh ch*urch); *rz* is *zh* (the French *J*acques). There are three specifically Polish vowels: *ą* is a nasal *o* (the French *on*); *ę* is a nasal *e* (the French fi*n*); *ó* (like *u*) is always *oo* (s*oo*t); as well as six consonants: *ć* (and *c* followed by *i*) is a soft (palatal) *ts* (a little like the Italian *c*iao); *ł* is *w* (*w*ood); *ń* (and *n* followed by *i*) is a palatalized *n* (the Spanish *ñ*); *ś* (and *s* followed by *i*) is a soft (palatal) *s*; *ź* (and *z* followed by *i*) is a voiced *ś* (plea*s*ure); and, finally, *ż* is, like *rz*, *zh* (the French *J*acques).

ABBREVIATIONS AND
SPECIALIZED TERMS

AK. Armia Krajowa, the Army of the Homeland (as opposed to the Army Abroad, in Great Britain and in the Soviet Union); the Polish armed underground movement aligned with the Polish government-in-exile.

Aktion. German euphemism for the transportation to Treblinka and the destruction of some 300,000 people from the Warsaw ghetto (July 22– September 15, 1942), also referred to as the "Resettlement" (*Umsiedlung*).

Annexed Territories. Polish prewar districts of Danzig, Pomerania, Silesia, Poznań, and Łódź incorporated into the German Reich in October 1939. For the rest of the Polish territories occupied by the Germans, see **GG.** All the Jews (with exception of a number in the Łódź district) and all the members of the Polish intelligentsia were expelled from the Annexed Territories to the GG at the begining of 1940.

Biuletyn ŻIH. *Biuletyn Żydowskiego Instytutu Historycznego* the *Bulletin of the Jewish Historical Institute.*

Bleter far Geshikhte. The *Historical Papers,* a Yiddish-language publication of the ŻIH.

Blue police. Policja Granatowa (named after the color of their uniforms), Polish police in the GG under the control of the *Ordnungspolizei* (Order police).

B.V.M. The Blessed Virgin Mary.

Caritas. Sometimes spelled Charitas. Catholic charitable organization. In the ghetto its head was Monsignor Marceli Godlewski.

Closed quarter, or the **quarter.** *Dzielnica zamknięta,* the usual wartime term for the ghetto.

"Endek." Member of the National Democratic Party; see **ND.**

Gazeta Żydowska. The *Jewish Gazette.* Polish-language German newspaper published in Cracow and directed at Jews.

GG. General Government (*Generalgouvernement*). The Polish districts of Cracow, Radom, Warsaw, Lublin (and after June 1941 also Lwów [Lvov]) governed directly by the German administration. Hans Frank was the general governor and Ludwig Fischer was the Warsaw district governor.

Gmina. See *Judenrat.*

Jewish Order Service. The Jüdischer Ordnungsdienst, Jewish ghetto police affiliated with the *Judenrat,* headed by Józef Szeryński and later by Jakub Lejkin.

JHK. See ŻSS.

Judenrat. German for "Jewish council." Set up by the Germans to organize all facets of the life in the ghetto and to implement Nazi orders. Known in the ghetto as *Gmina* or *Kehilla,* Polish and Hebrew respectively for "community," short for "community council."

Kehilla. See *Judenrat.*

Lebensunwertes Leben. "Life unworthy of living." Nazi euphemism describing physically and mentally handicapped persons slated for euthanasia in Germany and in the GG.

Left Po'alei Zion. Left faction of the Workers of Zion Party. In Poland the "Left" faction was strongly Marxist but not Communist in outlook.

Mekhes. Convert to Chritianity. Yiddish term, apparently from Hebrew, unknown to Yiddish speakers outside the Polish areas.[1]

ND. Stronnictwo Narodowo Demokratyczne, the National Democratic Party. A right-wing conservative party which, on the whole, considered Polish Jews as members of a foreign nation.

Nowy Kurier Warszawski. The *New Warsaw Courier.* Polish-language German newspaper published in Warsaw and directed at Poles.

Obmann. German for "chairman," the usual title of the head of the *Judenrat.*

---

1. The term is probably of Hebrew origin, but its etymology is far from established. *The Dictionary of the Polish Language* (*Słownik Języka Polskiego*) (Warsaw: Polska Akademia Nauk, 1962) offers: "meches, a Jew who became a Christian [żyd, który przyjął chrześciaństwo] from Hebrew = payment, custums duty [opłata, cło]" (4:546). This etymology seems to be doubtful on semantic grounds. Uriel Weinreich, *Modern English Yiddish and Yiddish English Dictionary* (New York: McGraw-Hill, 1968), does not offer etymologies, and does not list *mekhes,* although he lists a more semantically satisfactory verbal form: "MAKKhESH deny, recant" (546). But the Hebrew etymon remains elusive.

Oneg Shabbath. Yiddish form: Oyneg Shabbes. A cryptonym for the Ringelblum Archives of the ghetto, containing two collections of documents: Ring I and Ring II.

ONR. Obóz Narodowo Radykalny, the Radical National Camp. An extreme Polish nationalist and anti-Semitic party founded in 1934. It was outlawed by the Polish government, but it had a strong following among university students.

Ordnungsdienst. See Jewish Order Service.

Ordnungspolizei. The German Order police in Warsaw.

Pawiak. A large prison so called because it was situated on Pawia Street, in the northern part of the ghetto.

Po'alei Zion. See Left Po'alei Zion.

PZPR. Polska Zjednoczona Partia Robotnicza, the Polish United Workers Party, the Communist party. Founded as the PPR (Polish Workers Party) in 1942 to replace the Polish Communist Party, dissolved by Stalin. The PZPR, aligned with the Soviet Union, ruled Poland between 1945 and 1989.

Quarter. See Closed quarter.

Resettlement. See *Aktion*.

Resettlement Staff. Umsiedlungsstab, a special group of German officers created in July 1942 to direct the *Aktion*.

RGO. Rada Główna Opiekuńcza, the Main Welfare Council. The only Polish social agency tolerated by the Germans. Its main tasks were caring for indigents and for refugees from the Annexed Territories. Adam Ronikier was the head of the RGO.

Ring I. See Oneg Shabbath.

Ring II. See Oneg Shabbath.

"Ronikiers." The name given to those prominent Christianized Jews who in late 1939 asked the RGO to clarify their status. They were exempt from wearing armbands and from living in the Jewish quarter until the beginning of 1941, when they were arrested and forced into the ghetto.

Seuchensperrgebiet. German for "Closed area of epidemic." The early designation of the area that would become the ghetto.

Szmalcownik. Polish term for a blackmailer and extortionist of money from Jews in hiding (lit. "grease seeker").

Umschlagplatz. German for "transfer place." This term, usually shortened to *Umschlag,* was never translated either into Yiddish or into Polish. A railway siding situated on Zamenhof and Niska Streets in the northern part of the ghetto. Some 300,000 Jews were loaded onto trains there during the *Aktion* and shipped to Treblinka.

Umsiedlung. See *Aktion.*

Volksdeutsch. "Ethnic German," a Polish citizen of German origin who accepted conditional German citizenship after October 1939.

WSM. Warszawska Spółdzielnia Mieszkaniowa, the Warsaw Housing Cooperative, a truly liberal housing, health, and educational association, active chiefly in the northern quarter of Warsaw called Żolibórz, counting among its members many assimilated or Christianized Jews.

YHK. See ŻSS.

YIVO. Yiddishe Visenshaftlikhe Organizatsie (Institute for Jewish Research), founded in Vilna and transfered to the United States after the war.

Żegota. Cryptonym for Rada Pomocy Żydom, the Council for Aid to Jews, organized in the fall of 1942 with considerable financial assistance from the Polish government-in-exile (London).

ŻIH. Żydowski Instytut Historyczny, the Jewish Historical Insitute in Poland, on Tłomackie Street in Warsaw, containing a museum, archives, library, and publication house.

ŻOB. Żydowska Organizacja Bojowa, the Jewish Fighting Organization, founded in the summer of 1942 for the coming armed struggle and composed of Bund members, left Zionists, and communists. The ŻOB was the main fighting organization in the ghetto uprising.

ŻSS. Żydowska Samopomoc Społeczna, the Jewish Mutual Aid Committee. The ghetto body overseeing all Jewish social and charitable institutions in the GG. Michał Weichert was the chairman. The Yiddish acronym was YHK (the Polish transcription, JHK).

Zwangsgesellschaft. German for "coerced society," such as existed in concentration camps and in the Warsaw Ghetto.

ŻZW. Żydowski Związek Wojskowy, the Jewish Military Union. Military wing of the right-wing Zionist Revisionist Youth, organized in October 1942. Fought in the Ghetto uprising.

CHAPTER ONE

Autobiographical and Other Reasons for Writing This Book

I was born in Warsaw in December 1925. I spent most of the war years in Warsaw, where I was educated in the clandestine high school (secondary education being forbidden for Poles). More important, just before I turned seventeen, I became active in the Polish underground army (Armia Krajowa, henceforth AK). I was arrested on April 7, 1944, during a general roundup involving a house-to-house search and verification of documents. I was sent to the infamous prison known as Pawiak (an old Russian-built prison on Pawia Street in the northern part of what was to become the ghetto). I was released on May 3, after my organization managed to bribe one of the corrupt Gestapo officials. Later, I participated in the Polish uprising, August 1 to October 2, 1944, and after the capitulation I became a prisoner of war (Stalag XB, Sandbostel, no. 221 857). Liberated by the British, I spent some time in the Polish army in Italy. Like many of my generation, I did not wish to return to Poland, which by then was run by the Communists, who made clear their animosity to former soldiers of the AK. At the end of 1946 I went to Canada on a two-year contract as a farm laborer. In 1948 I began my university studies in British Columbia and continued graduate studies in Paris and at the University of California in Berkeley, where I received a Ph.D. in Romance philology and medieval French in 1960. Since then I have been a professor, and I have spent the last thirty-six years at the University of Chicago. I became an emeritus professor in 1995, but I continue to teach part-time.

Both my parents belonged to the Polish intelligentsia. Both of them were descendants of small landowners who had lost their possessions in the former Russian part of Poland (my father's family in the 1880s, my mother's in 1922). My father, Włodzimierz Dembowski, was a lieutenant in the Polish army. In the last years of his life, he became an officer in the border guards. He died of a heart attack in 1937 at the age of forty-four.

My parents were very patriotic, having grown up in the atmosphere of the underground struggle for Polish independence. They both came from a rather typical intelligentsia background; their ideology was based on their faith in progress, science, education, democratic socialism, and, above all, national independence. Like many in their class, they were more or less indifferent to the religious aspects of life. They considered religion an antiquated and antiintellectual ideology, good perhaps for the lower classes. Just before her marriage, however, my mother, Henryka Sokołowska, became a seriously committed Christian. Although my father could not accept a personal religious commitment, he had always been scrupulously ethical. Like many of his background and generation, he lived in the ethical legacy of Christianity without realizing it. There was absolutely nothing antireligious in his attitudes. Thus before their marriage he promised my mother that he would participate in the Christian upbringing of his children. He always observed this promise in fact and in spirit.

After my father's sudden death in 1937, my mother had a difficult time caring for her five children, and she was obliged to distribute three of us among our relatives. From 1938 through the war, I lived with various relatives, but chiefly with the family of my paternal uncle, Kazimierz Dembowski, and his wife, Janina Landy Dembowska. This situation was temporary at first, but when my mother and my sister Małgorzata were arrested on the night of May 14, 1941, it became permanent.

The circumstances of their arrest were typical of the period. One night when my mother was visiting Warsaw, she missed her transportation back to the village where she lived. Caught by the curfew, she had to spend the night in Warsaw with my father's sister Aniela Sierakowska. There was a Jewish woman who used to live as a registered tenant in Aniela's apartment before the establishment and closing of the ghetto. German police (*Ordnungspolizei*) came to inquire about this tenant, or probably to arrest her if she were still there. When they found my mother they thought that she might be this Jewish tenant. During the process of establishing her identity (*Grundsätze*), my mother mentioned her daughter and furnished her address, probably to prove her own identity. At the last moment, one of the more inquisitive policemen looked into her suitcase and found a considerable quantity of underground newspapers (my mother was a regular courier for the underground press).

After about four months in the Pawiak prison, my mother and sister were sent to Ravensbrück—a concentration camp for women—and executed there on September 25, 1942.

I learned these facts only after the war from the surviving women, including Aniela. From May 1941 on, I became even closer to my aunt, Janina, and after the disappearance of my mother she became my true parent. In the 1960s, when the Polish Communists became less pronounced in their anti-AK animus—at least against former rank-and-file members—I visited Janina several times in Poland, and in 1967 she came to Chicago for a few weeks. It was only then that we had long conversations about the "bad old days," and it was only then that I learned much about her background. Just before she died, in 1979, I paid my last visit to her to Poland, and I promised her that I would write about Jewish Christians or Christian Jews.

Janina Landy was born in 1896 to a distinguished Jewish-Polish family. She was one of the four children of Władysław and Anna Muszkat Landy. Janina's brother Adam became an prominent member of the illegal Polish Communist Party. He was not the only extreme leftist in the family. A maternal cousin, Zofia, married the (in)famous "Iron Feliks" Dzierżyński, the creator of the Soviet secret police under Lenin.

All the members of the Landy family spoke with pride about their ancestor Michał Landy. During an anticzarist demonstration in 1861, the young Michał marched right behind the cross-bearing leader of the demonstration. The Cossacks fired on the crowd, killing the leader. Michał Landy picked up the cross and was wounded in turn. He died a few days later and was buried in the Jewish cemetery in Warsaw. In a recent discussion of Jewish history, Stanisław Krajewski describes the death of Michał Landy as one of the "instances where the Jewish-Polish cooperation took on a form so profound that it became symbolic" (1998, 75; see also Morawska 1960–61). Janina, more mystically, always looked on her ancestor's death as a foreshadowing of her own conversion.

Janina's two younger sisters, Zofia and Henryka, became Christians shortly after her own conversion in 1915. Zofia Landy became an important neo-Thomist, a publicist, and a Franciscan nun. Janina, trained in literature, was an excellent teacher and later the principal of a private high school for girls. If Janina instilled in me a love of learning and respect for knowledge, I owe her sister, Henryka Landy Martyniak, one of the best teachers of French in Poland, my proficiency in the French language, as well as my interest in all things French. Part of Janina's extended family settled permanently in France. It was there that she was baptized in 1915. The next day, she married my paternal uncle, Kazimierz Dembowski. The baptism was obviously not motivated by the desired marriage. Kazimierz, like my father, was neither religious nor antireligious.

To help my memory in recalling all that is to be known about the Landy family, I shall quote a passage of a book written by a Polish educator, Maciej Demel. Its subject is Dr. Aleksander Landy, an outstanding pediatrician, a social activist, and Janina's paternal cousin. In this passage Demel offers his appreciation of Janina's brother and sister. We should remember that he is writing in 1982 from a distinctly left-wing but non-Communist point of view.

Adam and Zofia [Landy]. It is well to note the lives of those two. Adam Landy (1891–1937) represents the extreme left orientation. In his early youth, he participated in the School Strike [1905], and later became a leading member of the [illegal] Polish Communist Party and of the Profintern [Soviet-controlled International Labor Unions]. He was arrested several times in Poland and left for the USSR, where, in 1937, he became "the victim of the provocation" [this "politically correct" phrase means that he was executed in the Great Purges]. He was rehabilitated [by the Polish Party] in 1956.

Completely different—although equally difficult—was the career chosen by Zofia (1894–1972). At first she was an ardent Socialist like her parents, her brother, and her cousin, a romantic Siberian exile. But later she became—as is typical for many converts—an equally ardent fideist: she was very active in the Catholic Renewal Movement. She completed her philosophical studies in France, where she attended the lectures of such famous professors as Lévy-Bruhl and Durkheim at the Sorbonne, and Henri Bergson at the Collège de France. She became a friend of many leading European intellectuals, such as Jacques Maritain. In Warsaw, she became a leading member of the "Circle" [Kółko] of Rev. [Władysław] Korniłowicz as well as the leading contributor to the quarterly Verbum, which . . . in the years before World War II was a serious journal open to all sorts of philosophical and theological opinions. . . . In the 1920s Zofia and many of her friends from the "Circle" joined Mother Elżbieta Czacka, who had not only founded the Institute for the Blind in Laski [near Warsaw], but also a Franciscan Order [whose members would run the institute and take care of the blind]. She worked there under her new convent name of Sister Teresa, as a teacher of the blind. She continued her work as a neo-Thomist philosopher, a publicist and propagator of all that she believed and that she practiced, until an advanced age. (32–33)

I personally knew Aleksander Landy and Sister Teresa. In fact I spent part of 1938 in Laski, where Sister Teresa taught religion in grade 6 and where I was the only seeing pupil. Neither Janina's father, who died before the war, nor her mother, known to all as *babcia* or "granny," were Christians. They were assimilated Jews whose only religion, in Janina's words, was Polish patriotism. But *babcia* got along very well with her offspring and the members of their extended families, whether they were ardent Christians, ardent Communists, or ardent nonbelievers. She was arrested in one of the frequent Gestapo roundups and shot as a Jewess in 1943, I believe.

Before relating the "prehistory" of the Landy-Dembowski connection let me mention the fate of my maternal grandfather, for he was an essential part of this connection. Wojciech Sokołowski and his youngest daughter, Maria, perished as victims of yet another Nazi-sponsored annihilation program. This was a historical and logical foreshadowing of the Shoah: the destruction of the "life unworthy of living" (*lebensunwertes Leben*). Maria suffered from a birth trauma (forceps injury of the skull) and was placed in a state hospital when she became an adult. Her father chose to spend his retirement years living in one of the cottages on the hospital grounds, rented to relatives of the wards. Hitler signed a decree authorizing the removal of "incurables" dated September 1, 1939, although some euthanasia of that kind was practiced in the Reich before this decree. In occupied Poland, the new law was put in practice more quickly and with greater thoroughness than in the Reich. Wojciech and Maria were shot in October 1939 with all the other patients and their permanent visitors. I learned the details of their deaths only after the war.

The Landy family met the Dembowskis through marriage. In the very difficult years of 1917 and 1918, the young Zofia Landy (the future Sister Teresa) was a live-in tutor to my mother and her sisters at my maternal grandfather's estate. Kazimierz Dembowski was already married to Janina Landy. Through Zofia, Kazimierz became acquainted with the Sokołowski family. My father was captured on the Russian front as a member of the Polish Legion in the Austrian army. In 1918 he came to the Sokołowski estate to recuperate from the ravages caused by his Russian captivity and his wandering through a Russia torn by revolution and civil war. It was at the Sokołowski estate that my father met his future wife, Henryka, who under Zofia's influence had also become a devout Christian. On October 26, 1918, my father married my mother.

Zofia Landy and "her" Laski have thus always had a special place in our family. This relationship was strengthened by my mother's sister, Zofia Sokołowska. At more or less the same time that Zofia Landy became Sister Teresa, Zofia Sokołowska, a young sculptress of some renown, became Sister Katarzyna in Laski. And after World War II, my older sister Katarzyna became (logically enough) Sister Zofia. My brother, Rev. Bronisław Dembowski, was for many years a rector in the Warsaw convent church of the Laski Franciscans. After the fall of Communism in Poland, he became bishop of Włocławek but remained in close touch with Laski.

Janina, her sisters, and her very numerous friends—Christians, neo-Christians, or assimilated Jews—had a profound influence on my life. Many of them lived in close touch with the progressive and leftist (though usually non-Communist) circles in the northern district of Warsaw (Żoliborz), where the atmosphere was dominated by the Warsaw Housing Cooperative movement (Warszawska Spółdzielnia Mieszkaniowa, or WSM). The WSM had built several large apartment blocks which were occupied by the coop member-owners, usually from the liberal intelligentsia. Among them were a considerable number of assimilated Jews. The WSM was not just a housing cooperative; it was also a progressive and a politically sophisticated association with its own high school, an adult education program, and health services run by the Aleksander Landy. It was here, in this profoundly antifascist atmosphere, that people perhaps knew more about Hitler than in any other place in prewar Poland.[1] As Demel says: "The Żoliborz Left looked very soberly toward the future . . . they knew what fascism was. . . . In fact, the whole politically sophisticated WSM community did not have any illusions as to the true intentions of fascism" (1982, 90). This foresight was part of the reason why the December 1939 German law forcing Jews to wear Star of David armbands met with almost universal noncompliance among the Jews who, baptized or not, were connected to the WSM. People like the Landys did not even think about registering as Jews, which was not the case, as we shall see, with many other Jewish Christians.

My deep affection and feeling of gratitude toward Janina Landy Dembowska and her family and the promise that I made to her are my chief reasons for writing this book. But they are not the only reasons. Like many people of

---

1. In her testimony to Yad Vashem (no. 49E/5719), Danuta Dąbrowska (Jakoba Blidsztajn) stresses the extraordinary character of the WSM and specifically mentions that Dr. Aleksander Landy managed to acquire false "Aryan" papers for her. He and his wife Wanda (maternal aunt of Dr. Irena Kanabus) hid several Jews during that period.

my birthplace and my generation, I carry the burden of memory. Mine eyes have seen, and I remember. I remember, even if, as I said, I do not trust my memory about the details. I was in Warsaw in the terrible days of the ghetto.

Although the things I write about happened sixty years ago, I remember many of them. I remember the constant humiliation and mistreatment of the Jewish work gangs by their guards, especially in 1940, before the sealing off of the ghetto. I remember particularly one of the popular forms of entertainment practiced by the guards: they forced the Jewish workers to fight each other or to sing (in Polish) the song praising the "golden Hitler, who taught us how to work." I remember the German Polish-language propaganda posters: "Jew = Louse = Typhus."

Above all, I remember traveling in the no. 17 streetcar from the city center north to Żolibórz. The streetcar used to run from Krasiński Square and went along Bonifraterska Street. Until December of 1941, this last street was situated in the northeastern part of the ghetto (after that date the street became its eastern frontier, but much of the ghetto street was visible from the streetcar). The sight of skeleton-like men, women, and children, dying or dead of hunger on the street, haunts my memory to this day. One of my recurring nightmares—a typical dream of a bystander—has me riding the crowded no. 17 when suddenly somebody pushes me out onto Bonifraterska. Now I am one of "them."

I remember the scared and silent visitors who frequently came to Janina's apartment to spend a night or two. They were Jews "in hiding," but I learned very quickly not to inquire about their provenance and identity.

I remember perhaps with the greatest clarity my own arrest on April 7, 1944, Good Friday of that year. I was arrested during one of those round-ups and searches of several building blocks in the "red" Żolibórz. Some sixty of us were arrested, including perhaps eight Jewish men and women caught with "bad" papers or with no papers. We stayed together for a few hours in a transit cell in the Pawiak. We whispered. Later, "we" were turned into the Registrar's office and entered the regular prison, while "they" were led outside to the already destroyed ghetto. They knew and we knew that they would be shot that very day. That particular memory, the memory of my "automatic" reaction—"Thank God that I am not . . ."—has prevented me from ever forgetting the absolute distinction that existed in those terrible days between Jews and non-Jews.

Thus I can speak with a certain confidence about my memories, above all the memories of such strong and "ineffaceable" experiences. I am less confident about the veracity of less traumatizing personal memories. I am also skeptical about what others remember about these details. I have read many war memoirs written many years after the events recalled. Quite often, I found impossible "facts." One memoirist, for example, claims that he saw me, Piotr Dembowski, pseudonym "Syn," killed in the first days of August 1944.

Much has been written about personal recollections of horrors, about personal accounts in the now fashionable "oral history," including the collective memories of the Shoah. This is not a place to dwell on these very difficult theoretical and practical questions. But I wish to contribute one detail pertinent to the accuracy of much of the reminiscence literature, something specific about the memory of sixteen-to-nineteen-year-old members of the underground in 1940–44. As a part of their conspiratorial activities, they had to cultivate the virtue of not knowing. On the "Aryan"—and also, I believe, on the Jewish—side of the wall there was a systematic effort at not knowing, not wishing to know, what anybody else was doing. The principle of conspiracy was, "You cannot disclose under Gestapo interrogation what you do not know."

Thus, I knew vaguely that my older brother Franciszek was in the AK, but only much later during the war did I learn that he was in my own company. (He survived the war, but he went to a different prisoner of war camp.) Some persons that I knew very well were engaged in important wartime underground activities, but I learned about their activities only after the war, and even then not from them. In his book *The Pianist*, Władysław Szpilman talks about his two "Aryan" friends: the artists Andrzej Bogucki and his wife, who used her maiden name, Janina Godlewska. Godlewska was a former student of my aunt Janina and a very good friend of the family. Szpilman relates that in February 1943, Andrzej and Janina agreed to find him a safe house in a studio belonging to an absent colleague, and to lead him to that house after he had sneaked away from his work gang outside the ghetto. As Szpilman tells the story: "Bogucki was standing on the corner of Wiśniowa Street. . . . When he saw me he began moving off rapidly. I walked a few paces behind him. . . . Janina Godlewska was waiting for us in the studio: she looked nervous and fearful. On seeing us she breathed a sigh of relief" (1999, 132). I had met our friends Bogucki and Godlewska-Bogucka many times between February 1943 and July 1944, but I did not know anything about their role in rescuing Szpilman until I read about it in his memoir. Thus I can serve as a witness to their characters and to their lives in Warsaw in the war years, but not to the facts of their rescue activities. I should mention, however, something that adds poignancy to Szpilman's account. I know that Godlewska-Bogucka was an extremely nervous person. She lived in a constant state of fear of the Germans.

She simply was not one of those persons who are endowed with personal courage. In spite of her fears she acted bravely. Her action thus deserves far greater praise from those who knew her. Both she and her husband were awarded the medal of the Righteous among the Nations.

Another illustration of the "know-nothing" principle and its role in reminiscences is also mentioned briefly by Demel. Among Aleksander Landy's close associates was a Dr. Irena Kanabus, a relative of his. I remember her from before the war as one of those conscientious Żolibórz doctors, and as a sweet, blonde lady who used to come to treat my frequent colds. During the war I met her husband, a surgeon, a bright, good-humored, extremely energetic man, Dr. Zenon Feliks Kanabus. I suspected that he was participating in some illegal activity, because most of us were "involved." But only after the war did I learn that he was an important member of the clandestine Coordinating Committee of Democratic and Socialist Doctors and was active in an important kind of assistance to the Jews in hiding. Together with another physician, he performed plastic surgery to remove the effects of ritual circumcision, or if that was impossible, he issued false certificates stating that a recent operation performed for hygienic reasons had left scars identical to those of ritual circumcision. Dr. Zenon Kanabus and Dr. Irena Kanabus have been recognized as Righteous among the Nations, he in 1965 and she in 1995.[2]

In writing this book, then, I have used documents of all kinds, but I have interpreted them in the light of my own memories, of my own appreciation of the memories of others, and of my understanding of the circumstances in which these memories were published and disseminated under the Communist regime.

———

Besides my personal reasons for undertaking to write this book, there are other, more general ones. My microhistorical subject is those victims of the Shoah in Warsaw who are practically never mentioned outside Poland: the baptized Jews. I believe that had I returned to Poland in 1945 and continued living there all my life, I would not have to write this book. The existence of Christian Jews and their fate is relatively well known there, although much less so among the younger generation. But I am an American and an American academic. Virtually all my adult life has been spent in North American

---

2. I wish to thank Havi Ben-Sasson from the Yad Vashem Institute for supplying me with copies of the testimonies concerning Zenon and Irena Kanabus: by Professor Adam Drozdowicz (no. 3397/102–3) and by Danuta Dąbrowska (Jakuba Blidsztajn) (no. 49-E/5719).

universities, and I know that this particular aspect of the Shoah is unknown there. Since entering the academic world, I have asked the same question of the people with whom I discuss the Shoah. "Do you know that there were two or three Roman Catholic parishes, as well as Orthodox and Protestant Christians in the Warsaw ghetto?" The answer has always and without exception been "no." A Chicago colleague and friend who is very well acquainted with the history of the Shoah did not know anything about the Christians in the Warsaw ghetto except that the chief of the Jewish police in the ghetto was indeed a convert.

I wish to believe that my work might dispel this almost universal ignorance about the Christian communities in the ghetto. As we shall see, the converts and the assimilated Jews played an important role in the ghetto, and their presence there illustrates the truly unprecedented character of the Shoah. Their voices, and the voices of those who spoke about them, should be heard.

CHAPTER TWO

The Sources and Their Problems

Until Havi Ben-Sasson's recent article, "Christians in the Ghetto"—an informative and bibliographically rich introductory study written by a staff member of the International School for Teaching the Holocaust, Yad Vashem—there were no works in English specifically treating the presence of Christian Jews in the Warsaw ghetto. There are some documents available in Yiddish and in Polish, many of them preserved in the Jewish Historical Institute in Warsaw [Żydowski Instytut Historyczny, henceforth ŻIH]. Many of these documents, written in Polish or in Yiddish, or frequently Yiddish translated into Polish, were edited and published with important comments and annotations, but some of them still remain unpublished. Some Warsaw wartime documents contain specific information about Christian Jews, who are also mentioned quite often in the rich Polish postwar literature concerning the saving and hiding of Jews who managed to find themselves outside the ghetto. Much of this information is scattered throughout the Jewish and non-Jewish literature.

But there is no single, exhaustive monograph dedicated specifically to this subject. I know of only five rather short items. The first is a study entitled "Assimilationists and Neophytes at the Time of War-Operations in the Closed Jewish Quarter" written in Polish at the suggestion of Emanuel Ringelblum by an intelligent and informed person living in the ghetto. This report was composed shortly before the summer of 1942 by someone using the pseudonym Władko. Joseph Kermish later identified Władko as Marian Małowist and included his essay in his English edition of a collection of documents taken from the Ringelblum Archives.[1]

The four other works were written after the war in Polish: a short article by Iwona Stefańczyk, "Christian Jews in the Warsaw Ghetto" (1997); a brief section entitled "The Christians in the Ghetto," part of an informative and meticulously researched work by Ruta Sakowska (1993, 138–40); part of a chapter from a book written by two Polish literary historians and critics, Barbara Engelking and Jacek Leociak, "Catholic Jews in the Warsaw Ghetto" (2001, 620–24); and, finally, Marian Fuks's chapter "Christians in the Warsaw Ghetto," in his *From the History of the Great Catastrophe of the Jewish People* (1996, 63–67). Fuks is a former secretary of the publication board of the ŻIH and a social historian of Polish Jews who is himself a descendant of baptized Jews. Fuks's short chapter is important not so much for the facts presented as for his short personal digression, which I shall discuss in my last chapter.

Before addressing the general subject of available sources, I must touch on the complex problem of Communist attitudes toward the then recent events, especially in the years immediately following the war. Except among professional historians working on World War II and its aftermath, the problem is hardly known. The decisively unfriendly attitudes toward independent research into the history of that period influenced profoundly the creation, preservation, editing, and publication of documents dealing with the Shoah, as well as the study of such documents. Most archives were not open to scholars.

Many of the most active members of the underground anti-Nazi movement—the persons most knowledgeable about the historical facts and background—were persecuted in the late 1940s and early 1950s. One example will suffice: Władysław Bartoszewski, one of the most important organizers of

---

1. As chance would have it, I met "Władko," Marian Małowist, at the Institute for Advanced Study at Princeton, where we both spent a good part of the 1979–80 academic year. Since we had to maintain politically neutral relations as behooved the members of an international institute, we did not discuss the war or any other "Old Country" matters, for he was a party member and I an émigré. But I realized from our more "nonpolitical" conversations that from an early age Małowist had been a sincere and "believing" Marxist. By 1980, however, he, like many other Polish party members, was profoundly disenchanted by the regime of the Polish People's Republic. As a child he was crippled by polio, an infirmity complicated by the injuries suffered from being hit by a German army truck early in the war. He told me that, paradoxically, his physical handicap helped him to survive on the "Other Side," since it was difficult to imagine that an obvious cripple could be an escapee from the ghetto. He must have left the ghetto sometime in late 1942. Małowist survived the war to become professor of history at the University of Warsaw. He died in 1988.

aid to the Jews, as we shall see later, recognized as Righteous among the Nations, spent six years in a Communist prison for his active participation in the AK (Iranek-Osmecki 1972, 316–17).

The hostile attitude of the ruling Communists toward all forms of political life they did not or could not control resulted in their systematic censorship, which in turn led writers to continue their cautious wartime underground writing practices, resulting in self-censorship. I am convinced that this self-censorship had an even more negative influence on the establishment and preservation of archival collections and their scholarly interpretation than did the direct control and censorship. The testimony of Rev. Czarnecki is a case in point. As we shall see, he was a young priest who lived in one of the parishes in the ghetto until the *Aktion* in July 1942. This man, who knew everything about this parish, published, only in 1981, a brief note stressing chiefly the "professional," that is, pastoral, aspect of his parish. What a story he could have told!

This work is not the place to dwell on the relations of the Communist system with Jews, but in order to understand its attitudes toward Jews in general and toward the Shoah in particular, we must recall something quite often forgotten. The Soviet Communist movement had always been basically inimical to any "uncontrolled" groups, particularly religious groups. It is true that the Soviet Union recognized Jews as a separate nationality—in the sense of ethnicity—but their chief criterion for this classification was neither historical-traditional nor religious. Thus in the short-lived Jewish Autonomous Region, Birobidzhan, in the far eastern USSR, speaking Yiddish was a criterion of nationality. Until the end of the Soviet Union, there was no public discussion of a specifically Jewish Shoah. This persistent Soviet attitude profoundly influenced the local ruling parties of the People's Republics.

In Poland, however, the Communists could not ignore the Shoah as methodically as their Soviet protectors did, because half of the European Jewish population was within its pre-1939 borders, and because annihilation centers such as Auschwitz, Treblinka, Sobibor, Majdanek, Bełżec, and Chełmno nad Nerem (Ger. Kulmhoff) were located in its territory. Poland had to compromise. In fact the Polish Communists permitted, or, more precisely, did not prevent, the publication of some documents and studies dealing specifically with the Shoah.

The Third Reich Policy in Occupied Poland, for example, a broad historical work by Czesław Madajczyk completed in 1967, is written from a properly pro-Soviet point of view (1970: 1:12, 6). But in the introduction the author clearly acknowledges the rich historiographic contributions by Polish Jews publishing in Poland and abroad on the tragedy of the Polish Jews and the Poles of Jewish origin. Madajczyk considers the fate of the Jewish community both as a fragment of the great European tragedy of the Jews and as an integral part of the history of the Polish state under occupation. Two chapters in particular offer detailed analyses of the Shoah in Poland: chapter 31, "The Situation of the Jewish Population," and chapter 34, "The Final Solution."

As long as the government of the PZPR (Polish United Workers Party [Communist]) ruled Poland (1944–89), it followed with greater or lesser perspicacity and rigor the policy of "control of past events," a policy, needless to say, imposed on the government by the Soviet Union. The Communists looked askance at public discussion of certain historical facts, all of them touching on Jews, the chief of them being, of course, the 1939–41 Soviet occupation of the eastern part of prewar Poland. But many other subjects were treated as taboo: anti-Semitism, especially among working-class people; the preponderant role played by the AK in the anti-German resistance; Jewish political activities other than those under Communist control, among others. Thus there developed a general reluctance not only to publish studies about these issues but even to discuss them. This is how Jarosław Anders, a member of the postwar generation, puts it: "I discovered also the existence of a peculiar zone of silence surrounding everything that touched upon Polish-Jewish relations, especially during World War II. There were no books on the subject, no serious historical studies, no archives open to researchers. The issue barely existed in postwar Polish literature and art." Anders goes on to point out that this blank spot "encompassed not only officially sanctioned speech, but also private conversation with parents, neighbors, and trusted older friends" (2001, 36). We can replace the term "Polish-Jewish relations" by "Jewish fate," and the author's opinion would, it seems to me, be equally valid.

Certain concrete developments in the official policies of the Polish Communist government influenced the study of the Shoah. The history of the ŻIH in Warsaw can throw some light on these policies. The ŻIH houses important archives concerning the fate of the Jews from the entire territory of pre-1939 Poland. For our purpose here, the most important part of the holdings is the "Oneg Shabbath" or the Ringelblum Archives, which we will discuss shortly. The ŻIH was established in 1947, when it replaced the Central Jewish Historical Commission, founded in Lublin in 1944. The first years of the ŻIH's existence were devoted to research and testimonies with a view to the extradition of war criminals. In the 1950s and 1960s, the real historical work was the publication of important historical monographs concerning the Jews in Poland. More important for my subject here, many source materials were transcribed and published by the ŻIH, often by the Yiddish-language publishing house Yiddish Bukh, or in the journal *Bleter far Geshikhte* (since 1948), as well as in the Polish-language *Biuletyn ŻIH* (since 1951), where many important articles and source materials have appeared.

By 1968, however, relations between the Soviet Union, its satellites, and the state of Israel had been worsening for several years; the PZPR purged itself of Jews, now called Zionists, and subsequently adopted the more anti-Semitic stance now taken by the Communist government of Poland. As a result, many collaborators of the ŻIH emigrated. Both research and publication suffered. New publications began to appear in 1975, and the *Bleter far Geshikhte* came back to life only in 1980. The *Biuletyn ŻIH* did manage to publish through those years, although from December 1968 through 1973 the *Biuletyn* appeared without the names of the members of the publication board.

These conditions prevalent in the People's Republics had, of course, a profound influence on the publication and diffusion of the most important documents concerning our subject. Any researcher consulting the works published in Communist-controlled Poland must take into consideration the conditions under which a given document was published. Some very important works, as we shall see, had to wait for many years to be published.

———

Before I discuss the available documents, let us take a closer look at the lives of the chief authors of the ghetto memoirs and the fate of their works. The specific content of their work, especially that pertaining to the Christian Jews, will be presented in chapters 5 and 6.

Emanuel Ringelblum (1900–1944) received a Ph.D. with a dissertation on the early history of the Jews in Warsaw. He was connected with the Institute for Jewish Research in Vilna (Yiddishe Visenshaftlikhe Organizatsie, or YIVO), which attracted many Left Po'alei Zion members. At the beginning of the war, he was an established and highly productive historian of Polish Jewry. He became a leading figure in the cultural life of the ghetto and the spiritual father of the resistance.[2] He organized the underground archives of the ghetto under the code name of "Oneg Shabbath" (Yiddish: Oyneg Shabbas), which means "celebrants of the Sabbath," or literally "delightful Sabbath" (Isaiah 58:13). These collections of documents are also now known as

2. For a brief introduction to the life and works of this truly remarkable man, see Kermish's introduction to Ringelblum 1992, vii–xxvi. Ringelblum wrote this work when he was hiding on the "Aryan" side.

the Ringelblum Archives. The archives contain many documents of different kinds: letters received in the ghetto, German decrees, German posters, some diaries, and, most important, reports and memoranda as well as literary and artistic works gathered or solicited and obtained by Ringelblum from scores of collaborators.

Ringelblum saw to it that his archives were well hidden. The story of their preservation and discovery reads like a detective novel. The first part of the archives was placed in ten metal boxes and buried in the basement of the Hallmann Workshop (a manufacturing plant in the ghetto working for the Germans) on August 3, 1942. The workshop was lodged in a school building at 58 Nowolipki Street. The second part of the archives was buried in the same workshop in two large milk cans at the end of February or the beginning of March 1943. The third part was hidden by Marek Edelman at another manufacturing plant, at 34 Świętojerska Street. After the war these hidden treasures were covered by tons and tons of rubble, and the discovery of the metal boxes, in September 1946, and the milk cans, in December 1950, is almost miraculous. The third part of the Oneg Shabbath Archives was never discovered. The discovered materials, some of them damaged by water, were given to the ŻIH for preservation, copying, and eventual publication.[3]

At the end of February 1943, Ringelblum managed to escape from the ghetto with his wife, Judyta, and their son Uri. They were hidden with some thirty other persons in a specially constructed underground shelter, called "Krysia" (little Christine) which is also a pun on the Polish *kryć* "to hide." This shelter was constructed under the garden belonging to Władysław Marczak and his family with the help of the gardener Mieczysław Wolski (pseudonym Władysław), at 81 Grójecka Street in Warsaw.

Just before the ghetto uprising on April 19, 1943, Ringelblum returned to the ghetto and was caught by the Germans and deported to the Trawniki concentration camp. This was not an annihilation camp, but a work camp. The secret Polish organization Żegota received the news that he was in the camp only in July 1943, by means of a postcard sent under Ringelblum's false name: Rydzewski. After two unsuccessful attempts to free him, a Polish railroad employee, Teodor Pajewski (pseudonym Teodor), a member of the AK, and a young Jewish woman, Shoshanah Kossower (pseudonym Emilka), suc-

---

3. My account of the fate of the archives follows Sakowska (1980, 16–17); see also her shorter essay in English: Sakowska (2001). For Ringelblum's own appraisal of the establishment and activities of Oneg Shabbath, see Kermish (1986, 2–21).

ceeded in bringing Ringelblum back to Warsaw dressed in the uniform of a railroad employee.

A word about Żegota: It was a cryptonym for a secret organization set up to aid the Jews. Under the auspices of the underground delegate of the Polish government-in-exile (Delegatura), a special institution, the Council for Aid to the Jews (Rada Pomocy Żydom), was organized in Warsaw in the fall of 1942, with branches in the occupied Poland. Żegota included representatives of many groups and parties, but not the Communists. The "founding parents" and moving spirits were Władysław Bartoszewski and a writer, Zofia Kossak-Szczucka, the first chairman of the committee; both were named "Righteous among the Nations." The most pressing and immediate need for persons in hiding was funds for subsistence. Antony Polonsky estimates that "between 1942 and the end of the war [the Polish government-in-exile] granted [Żegota] nearly 29 million zlotys (more than $5 million), which it used for a few thousand Jewish families in Warsaw, Lwów (Lvov), and Kraków" (2001, 492).[4]

Shortly after his rescue, Ringelblum returned to the underground shelter, where he continued his historical work. Unfortunately, on March 7, 1944, the Gestapo, following a denunciation, discovered the shelter. Ringelblum, his family, some thirty other Jewish men, women, and children, Mieczysław Wolski and his nephew and helper, Janusz Wysocki, as well as a non-Jewish midwife who just happened to be assisting at a birth in the shelter were taken to Pawiak prison. "The Jews were shot soon after in the ruins of the destroyed ghetto, and no traces of Wolski and Wysocki were ever found. Posthumously [both were] awarded the medal of 'Righteous among the Nations'" (Juszkiewicz et al. 1993, 81–82).[5] There is a sad epilogue to this tragic story: "In Warsaw the 18-year-old Gestapo informer, one Jan Łakiński, was condemned to death by the Tribunal of the Underground and executed. He is thought to have denounced the people hidden with Emanuel Ringelblum and his family" (Godlewski and Krzysztofowicz 1974, 99).

4. Sakowska (1980, 17–18) calculates that there were more than 4,000 Jews in hiding assisted by Żegota in Warsaw alone. See also Kermish in the postscript to his edition of Ringelblum (1992, 293–301). There is a lively account, containing many individual testimonies, of the activities of Żegota in Tomaszewski and Werbowski (1994). Individual Communists and their groups helped many Jews in hiding, but I do not know of any coordinating efforts inside the Communist underground.

5. The midwife is mentioned by Sakowska (1980, 18–19), but she also says that, in addition to Wolski and Wysocki, the Marczak family was taken and shot, which is incorrect.

In the short time spent in "Krysia," Ringelblum was typically very busy. He wrote a memorandum, now lost, about the Trawniki camp, and the essay *Polish-Jewish Relations*. This essay, while treating matters mostly outside the scope of our subject, contains a short passage about the "neophytes," that is, men or women baptized as adults. The publication history of this essay is typically complex. The original Polish was published only in 1988, whereas the first English translation appeared in 1976.

Ringelblum also kept a journal in the ghetto. The Yiddish manuscript of this journal was hidden in one of the metal containers together with the other documents of the Oneg Sabbath. Because of its crucial importance for the history of the Warsaw ghetto, the publication of the fragments of the journal in the original Yiddish was undertaken by the ŻIH as early as 1948. It was published in installments in *Bleter far Geshichte* in the volumes for 1948, 1951, 1952, and 1958 under the title *Notitsn fun varshever geto* (Notes from the Warsaw ghetto). Large parts of the *Notitsn* were translated into Polish and published in installments in the *Biuletyn ŻIH* in the volumes of 1951, 1952, 1954, and 1955. The incomplete, hastily prepared, and, I believe, heavily censored *Notitsn* were published in book form in 1952,[6] and about ten years later the ŻIH published these *Notes* under a new title, *Togbukh fun varsherver geto* (Journal from the Warsaw ghetto) as volume 1 of a far more careful two-volume edition of all Ringelblum's writing entitled *Ksovim fun geto* (Writings from the ghetto; 1961). A team of scholars from the ŻIH proceeded to prepare an annotated Polish translation of the 1961 Yiddish text. The completed text was deposited with the Czytelnik publishing house in 1963. But the *Chronicle of the Warsaw Ghetto . . . (Kronika getta warszawskiego . . .)* was to gather dust for a quarter of a century, until 1988.[7] The events in Poland of 1968 and their repercussions almost certainly played a role in that delay, but nothing could account for the full twenty-five years of delay except the prevailing ill will.

6. The date is important: the Communist effort to present its own version of history was at its peak. Kermish offers a severe critique, blaming the distortions in the 1952 *Notitsn* and the 1951–53 Polish translations on political censorship. He concludes: "We could indicate page by page countless tendentious admissions and irresponsible mistakes in the Warsaw editions of Ringelblum's manuscripts. But what was said above is sufficient to render an account of the great wrong that was done to the author, the martyr" (1953).

7. The Polish *Kronika* contains Ringelblum's journal entries between September 1939 and January 1943, and the fragments of "Silhouettes" (*Sylwetki*) of socially and culturally prominent Jews who died before Ringelblum left the ghetto.

Unlike the Yiddish *Togbukh* and Polish *Kronika* (abundantly footnoted and commented), the entire text of Ringelblum's journal is not available either in English or in any other Western European language. There is one incomplete translation, or rather a version of it, prepared by Jacob Sloan (Ringelbaum 1958). He published his work before the correctly transcribed 1961 Yiddish edition became available, and it is therefore based on the 1952 incomplete Yiddish book and on the other earlier publications. The Sloan edition is inadequate, both because of omissions in his source-text and because of errors made both by him and by his source-text. Let me offer one example of such omissions, concerning neophytes. Under the date December 24/25, 1941, Ringelblum writes: "Observers tell us that a great crowd of simple people, porters and such, come to the church on Leszno Street [the Church of the Nativity of the B.V.M.]. Numerous Jewish policemen see to it that they are not molested" (1988a, 324). This passage is absent from Sloan's English translation. Such omissions are made worse by Sloan's often misleading comments. For instance, in his afterword (346–47), he gives a completely inaccurate account of Ringelblum's death, in which his non-Jewish covictims are not mentioned.

Finally, Sloan's version is filled with translation errors. For example, in May 1940 Ringelblum notes that "they [the Germans] forcefully took blood from the children in a certain public [*powszechna*] school" (1988a, 139). The Polish term *powszechna*, "public," was used by Yiddish speakers to mean "public Polish-language school," which Sloan apparently did not know. Confusing the Yiddish *shul*, which means both "school" and "place of worship," Sloan translates the passage: "In a synagogue on Powszechna Street all the children were forced to give blood" (1958, 39). This is not an insignificant slip. To suggest that the Germans could have taken blood from Jewish children, despite their racial theories about blood, indicates a deep ignorance about the Warsaw ghetto and the horrible situation of the years 1939–43. Nor, of course, is there a Powszechna Street in Warsaw.

Sloan's translation was sharply and thoroughly criticized by Adam Rutkowski, an outstanding researcher at the ŻIH. Rutkowski cites a numbers of errors and reproaches Sloan with making all sorts of interpolations without indicating them as such. He points out that Sloan systematically either misspells Polish place-names, or instead of Polish names uses Yiddish place-names (Apt for Opatów, Ger for Góra Kalwaria, Raishe for Rzeszów, etc.) which cannot be found on an ordinary map. He mentions that Sloan wrongly transliterates personal names (the famous Dr. Korczak appears as Korczsak, Koreszak, Korscak) and misunderstands Polish currency and translates złoty as "piece of gold" or "guilder," and so on. The reviewer concludes, ". . . The adaptation by J. Sloan is a kind of a new work that has little to do with Ringelblum's text" (1963, 280).

Unfortunately, the shortcomings of the Sloan version were widely propagated, because it served as the source-text for the French, Italian, and Japanese translations.[8] For our purposes, Sloan's version and its offshoots are particularly inadequate because either his source-text or he himself left out many of Ringelblum's mentions of the neophytes. And the German book entitled *The Warsaw Ghetto: Journals from the Chaos* (see Ringelblum 1967) is not a translation of Ringelblum's journal at all, but in fact a translation of his other book, *Polish-Jewish Relations.*[9]

Obviously, some of the difficulties in the publication of Ringelblum's work stem from the very fact of their origin. It took much time to find, to decipher, and to transcribe these *Notitsn,* written in haste and, in a "conspiratorial" fashion, on small loose pieces of paper. But after 1961 the delays must be explained not only by technical difficulties but by the atmosphere in Communist Poland, which was politically unfriendly or bureaucratically hidebound or both.

Throughout this work, I shall cite either the passages in the *Notes* (Ringelblum 1958) checked against the Polish *Kronika* (Ringelblum 1988a), or my own translation of the Polish whenever the passage in question is absent or distorted in the *Notes.* Occasionally, I shall mention some differences between the Polish and English versions.

Whereas Emanuel Ringelblum's *Togbukh* is the chief document concerning Christian Jews written from a Jewish point of view, Dr. Ludwik Hirszfeld's Polish *The Story of a Life* (henceforth *Historia*) is the most important document written from a Christian vantage point (Hirszfeld, 2000). Hirszfeld, as we shall see, was an important scientist and a Christian convert. His *Historia* was written while he hid in the Polish countryside between June and August of 1943, with some additions written in 1944. It is divided into thirty-one chapters. The nine chapters that deal with Hirszfeld's life in the ghetto constitute the most important testimony about the Jewish Christians by a

8. French version: *Chronique du ghetto de Varsovie* (Paris, 1959); Italian version: *Sepolti a Varsavia. Apunti dal ghetto* (Milan, 1962); Japanese version: *Warshawa Ghetto: Hoshu 1940–42 no noto* (Tokyo, 1982).

9. Arieh Tartakower, who wrote an introduction for this work, cannot be blamed for the misleading title. His introduction treats Ringelblum's life: "Emanuel Ringelblum—der Historiker, der Kämpfer, der Martyr" (7–16). (While relating the death of Ringelblum and his family, Tartakower does not mention the death of other Jews and their non-Jewish protectors.)

Christian. After the war, the author wrote an epilogue especially for a planned American translation, but despite Hirszfeld's international status as a scientist, and despite the *Historia*'s importance for understanding life and death in the ghetto, this American edition never saw the light of day. The *Historia* has not been translated into any Western European language. The Western reader knows of some of Hirszfeld's activities in the ghetto only thanks to the book by Kazimierz Iranek-Osmecki (1972).

Ludwik Hirszfeld (1884–1954) was born in Warsaw.[10] He studied medicine in Germany before World War I and became a *Privatdozent* (unsalaried university lecturer) in Zurich. In 1915 he volunteered for service as a serological and bacteriological adviser to the Serbian army, which was being ravaged by epidemics of typhus and dysentery. He remained in Serbia and Greece throughout the war, and the memory of his activities there would always stay with him. Having left Poland when he was eighteen, he returned as a serious young scientist of thirty-five. In independent Poland, where he established a serum institute, he became the scientific head of the State Hygiene Institute in Warsaw and, later, a professor at the University of Warsaw. His achievements in biological fields made him world renowned. Working with a German colleague, he distinguished and named the blood groups O, A, B, and AB; a terminology quickly accepted by international institutions. In 1911 he discovered the inherited character of blood groups, which had far-reaching theoretical and practical applications. This man, who was to be dismissed by the Nazis because he belonged to the wrong "race," published with his wife (Hanna Kasman) a study in sero-anthropology which defined the racial composition of recent and historical people. In addition, he developed the theory of "serological conflict," later confirmed by the discovery of the Rh factor.

In the first days of the German occupation, Hirszfeld lost all his appointments. Quite late, on February 20, 1941, he was forced to move into the ghetto with his wife, Hanna, and their daughter, Maria (Marysia), who was suffering from tuberculosis.[11] There is a moving chapter in the *Historia* entitled "My Greatest Defeat" ("Moja największa przegrana") in which the disconsolate father speaks about Marysia's death in January 1943, or soon after: "All my life's work, all the goodwill I had gained, only sufficed so my twenty-three-year-old daughter could die in bed, surrounded by good and

10. This account of Hirszfeld's life is taken from Schadewaldt (1972).
11. As I mentioned in chap. 1, we lived in a small world. Before the war, Marysia Hirszfeld was a classmate and a friend of my first cousin, the younger daughter of Janina, Dr. Anna Dembowska Rodowicz.

friendly persons, so that she could be buried in her own grave, under a false name. For she had no right to live or to die under her own name" (434).

Hirszfeld was an important member of the medical establishment in the ghetto. Under the most difficult conditions, as one of the best qualified members of the Health Council, he organized antiepidemic measures and a vaccination campaign against typhus. He participated in retraining medical personnel and training students in 1941 and 1942. He knew many important personalities of the ghetto and he was well informed about the economic and health situation of the residents.

He and his family fled the ghetto at the end of July or the beginning of August 1942. The date 1943 given by Schadewaldt (1972), information probably found in the *Polish Dictionary of Biography,* is incorrect.[12] Hirszfeld states (2000, 274) that he arrived in the ghetto on February 3, 1941, and on p. 420 he speaks of "a year and half spent in the ghetto." He must have left the ghetto during the "Resettlement," that is, the deportations to the death camp of Treblinka, July–September 1942. Marysia died in the middle of January 1943 (Hirszfeld 2000, 432–34), obviously after some months outside the ghetto.

Once on the "Other Side," as the Polish quarter was known, the Hirszfeld family used a false name and, for security reasons, spread the rumor that all three of them had committed suicide. This rumor had tragic repercussions. In the United States Hirszfeld's colleagues and friends were ready to ransom him and his family from the hands of the Nazis, who were not averse to conducting such transactions, provided that the sums of money were high enough. Such sums were indeed collected in the United States, but when the International Red Cross notified the Americans that the Hirszfelds had committed suicide, the ransom proposal was withdrawn.

In the last period of the war, Hirszfeld and Marysia were hidden by several different people, mostly in a little village east of Warsaw. There he divided his time between taking care of Marysia and writing his memoirs. Hanna was working as a doctor in Warsaw, also under a false name.

Hirszfeld's autobiography is not a typical memorialist work from the Warsaw ghetto. A large part of the book deals with Hirszfeld's life before 1939. His sojourn in Serbia had earned him the undying gratitude of the Yugoslav authorities and, incidentally, the translation of his book into Serbian (Belgrad, 1962). More important, as a highly decorated member of the medical staff of the Serbian army in World War I, Hirszfeld received honorary Yugoslav citi-

---

12. See "Hirszfeld, Ludwik (1884–1954)," written by an anonymous member of the publication board.

zenship at the beginning of 1941 and an invitation to move there. Unfortunately, the Germans attacked Yugoslavia on March 27, 1941, and the invitation came to nothing. His autobiography treats events up until the summer of 1944, when the village where he was hiding was liberated by the Soviet army. He reported immediately to the new authorities and was appointed as one of the organizers of the new Maria Curie-Skłodowska University in Lublin. After the war he moved to Wrocław (Breslau) where he organized the medical school at the university and later created and directed the institute of Immunology and Experimental Therapy. After his death in 1954, the Institute was named after him. His funeral was attended by hundreds of mourners.

Another memorialist, Adam (Abraham) Czerniaków (sometimes written as Czerniakow) (1888–1942) was an engineer by profession and an educator by choice. He was born in an assimilated bourgeois family. Before the war, he was vice-chairman of the Jewish Confessional Community Council (Żydowska Gmina Wyznaniowa) in Warsaw. He also served as city councilor and was elected to the senate representing the coalition of the three Jewish conservative parties, Agudat Israel, Mizrahi, and the General Zionists. On September 23, 1939, during the siege of Warsaw, the Polish president of the city, Stefan Starzyński, appointed Czerniaków chairman of the Jewish Confessional Community Council, since the previous chairman, Maurycy Mayzel, had left Warsaw for eastern Poland in the first days of the war. On October 23, 1939, the German occupation authorities named Czerniaków head (*Obmann*) of the *Judenrat* (Jewish council). By force of habit, the population of the ghetto called the *Judenrat* by its traditional Hebrew name *Kehilla*, or *Gmina* in Polish. Here I use the terms Jewish Community Council or *Judenrat*.

Before the war the Jewish Confessional Community Council was an institution that regulated the educational and religious affairs of the Jews. In the ghetto, however, the *Judenrat* would become its internal self-government, whose main function would be to see to it that German orders and regulations were followed. Czerniaków would remain at this post, humiliated by the Germans and despised by the ghetto elite, such as Emanuel Ringelblum, and by the majority of its inhabitants, for serving the occupier. He believed that he could ameliorate the fate of his fellow ghetto dwellers. Czerniaków committed suicide on July 23, 1942, the second day of the "Resettlement."

His diary is quite different from the other memoirs. First of all, in comparison with, say, Ringelblum he was in a better material situation. He did not have to fight for his subsistence. Second, he was better informed than anybody else about the social and political situation inside and outside the ghetto. Although often duped by the German authorities, he knew more about them than most. Czerniaków was one of the assimilated Jews; he was a Polish patriot and a follower of Piłsudski, whose great portrait decorated his ghetto office to the last day. He had a distinctly literary turn of mind; he loved literature and wrote some verses and short stories in Polish. His diary, however, is written soberly and reads, as it was probably intended to be read, as personal notes hastily jotted down among constant occupations and preoccupations, notes to serve for a future book dealing with his experiences as chairman of the *Judenrat*.

Czerniaków's tragic position created a great deal of controversy after the war, and this delayed the publication of his journal. Ruta Sakowska sums up the controversy as follows:

> In the first years after the liberation, Czerniaków was branded not so much personally, but as the result of the general and negative stereotype of the *Judenrat*. His journal did not interest researchers. Only after its publication (in Israel, in 1968) did the controversy focus on the person and the activities of the Chairman of the Warsaw *Judenrat*. This controversy led, in Poland and elsewhere, to the idealization of the author and, indirectly, to the approval of the activities of the *Judenräte*. This is an erroneous position because this vindication, consciously or unconsciously, was accomplished at the expense of the resisting Underground circles of the Ghetto and in the first place, at the expense of Emanuel Ringelblum, who was considered the chief antagonist of the Chairman of the *Judenrat*. This continuing posthumous controversy was based not on personal prejudices, but rather on far more important matters—namely on the attitudes of the resisting circles, and of the general public to the *Judenrat*. (1993, 148)

The history of the publication and diffusion of the Czerniaków diary certainly reflects this long controversy. The manuscript, written in Polish, consists of eight copybooks. Originally there were nine, but one, containing the notes written between December 14, 1940, and April 22, 1941, was lost, probably when Czerniaków was interrogated by the Gestapo. Czerniaków's wife, Dr. Felicja Czerniakowa, escaped from the ghetto shortly after the death of her husband and was hidden in Warsaw among her "Aryan" friends. Their only son, the beloved Jaś, who is mentioned more than twenty times in the diary, left Warsaw for eastern Poland at the beginning of the war. He was deported to Kazakhstan by the Soviet authorities, where he died of hunger a few days before his father's suicide. I see in the deaths of father and son a symbol of the fate of the citizens of Poland, both Jews and non-Jews, during World War II—destruction on both fronts.

Sometime in 1947, Czerniaków's widow, finding herself in financial straits, offered to sell the manuscript of the diary to the ŻIH. ŻIH refused the offer because of its hostile attitude toward the *Judenrat* and Czerniaków. Later, Dr. Czerniakowa changed her mind about offering the manuscript to the ŻIH, because she thought that the memory of her husband had been slighted. Just before her death, she entrusted the manuscript to a cousin leaving for France. A person or persons in Canada sold it in 1964 to Yad Vashem. Thus Czerniaków's journal was published first in Hebrew with a facsimile of the original, then in the original Polish, and finally in English.[13]

Another important ghetto document which reflects the attitudes of its author—an educated and conservative Jew—toward the neophytes is the journal of Chaim Aron Kaplan (1880–1943). He was an outstanding Hebraist and the founder of a private Hebrew school. He was traditional in religion, conservative in politics, endowed with a critical mind, and decidedly disinclined to tolerate what he considered foolishness. From 1935 he kept a carefully written diary in Hebrew. In its last entry, written on August 4, 1942, Kaplan says, "If my life ends—what would become of my diary?" Kaplan died in Treblinka either in December 1942 or January 1943, but after many changes of fortune, the manuscript of his diary survived. Ringleblum knew Kaplan and tried to include Kaplan's diary in his archives, but only a small part of it was copied and housed in the Oneg Shabbath collection. During the "Resettlement" Kaplan entrusted the rest of the manuscript, written in several small copybooks, to a friend who worked on the "Other Side." One by one the friend smuggled the notebooks out of the ghetto and, in turn, entrusted them to a Pole, Władysław Wojcek, who kept in contact with the ghetto conspirators. Later, in 1952, Wojcek was instrumental in discovering the second part of Oneg Shabbath Archives.

Wojcek buried Kaplan's notebooks in a metal can on his father's farm. Only in 1952—one had to be prudent in Stalinist Poland—did Wojcek give the director of the ŻIH the notebooks containing parts of the diary for 1940 and 1941. In 1962 Wojcek emigrated to the United States. Armed with a letter of introduction from the ŻIH, he contacted Professor Abraham Katsh,

---

13. Information concerning the manuscript comes from Fuks's introduction to the Polish edition (Czerniaków 1983, 14–15). All the editions mentioned here are listed in the bibliography. The Polish version; edited by Fuks, first appeared in *Biuletyn ŻIH*, no. 83–84 (1972): 1–282. My citations are to the 1999 English version.

who purchased the notebooks in Wojcek's possession for the New York University Library's Jewish Cultural Foundations of Judaica and Hebraica collection. Jacek Leociak, whose summary of this complicated story I follow here, doubts Wojcek's explanations that he did not have enough time to hand the rest of the notebooks to the ŻIH. Rather, Leociak believes that Wojcek needed financial help in his new immigrant life.

Katsh translated and edited the parts of Kaplan's diary contained in the New York University notebooks. That edition, published in 1965, lacked thirteen crucial ghetto months: from April 4, 1941, to May 2, 1942. A second and complete edition was eventually published in 1973. Katsh explains in the introduction to this new edition that he obtained the missing parts of the diary from Yisrael Gutman of the Moreshet (the Mordachai Anilewitz Memorial Institute), in Israel. It is not clear how these missing parts had reached Israel, but anyone working with such documents knows better than to expect their history to be free of any blank spots.[14]

Another example—baffling for the uninitiated but quite understandable for those who know how much the Communists were obsessed with political correctness in general and with the control of history in particular—is the book *On the War between Mighty Germany and the Jews of Warsaw*, composed by a still unidentified person hiding on the "Other Side." It is signed with the pseudonym Stefan Ernest. Although the manuscript somehow found its way into the collection of the ŻIH, it was published in toto only in 2003.[15]

Ernest was a thoroughly assimilated, nonreligious Jew. We know that he was born in Warsaw, that he was well educated and had a good command of foreign languages, but not of Yiddish. He was an official in the Jewish Employment Service (Jüdische Arbeitsdienst) He was dismissed from his post in late 1942 and left the ghetto on January 29, 1943, by escaping from a detachment working outside the ghetto. He wrote his work in May 1943, during the final destruction of the ghetto, while hiding in the German quarter of Warsaw. Ernest writes very little about himself, about religion, Jewish or Christian, or about Christianized Jews, but he does offer his own highly individual views of the assimilationists and baptized Jews living on Sienna Street. This lucid account of Jewish ghetto society offers incisive but not necessarily condemnatory analyses of the chief personalities of the *Judenrat*. This, combined with

14. This new edition was reprinted by Indiana University Press in 1999, and my citations are to this reprint.

15. Some fragments of this work were published in Michał Grynberg's collection in 1988 (in Polish) and in 2002 (English).

the absence of any "left" political bias, explains why his book could not have been published during the era of the pro-Soviet government in Poland, but it is not clear why its publication occurred only in 2003. We do not know who Stefan Ernest was, nor do we know whether he survived after May 1943, or how his work found its way to the ŻIH.

Many other publications concerning both the Shoah in Poland in general and in the Warsaw ghetto in particular suffered a strange fate. Another typical, and by now much better known, example is the previously mentioned memoir of Władysław Szpilman. The fate of this memoir, which does not mention Christian Jews in the ghetto, clearly reflects the prevailing postwar atmosphere of censorship. Unlike Ernest's memoir, this politically innocent account written by a well-known musician employed by the Polish radio was published in Polish in 1946. The only "political incorrectness" of the book could have been the presentation of a good German, even if in the first edition he was called an Austrian. Wolf Biermann describes the book's subsequent history. Biermann is a reliable witness to events in the People's Republics. The son of a Jewish-German Communist killed at Auschwitz in 1943, Biermann lived in East Germany from 1945 to 1976. His literary works were banned in 1965, and he emigrated to the West in 1976. Here is his account in his epilogue to the 1999 English edition of *The Pianist,* itself based on a new and uncensored Polish text (2000): "[Szpilman's] book was published in Poland in 1946 under the title of one of its chapters, *Death of a City* [*Śmierć miasta*]. It was very soon withdrawn from circulation by Stalin's Polish minions. . . . As the countries conquered by the Red Army gradually became more firmly caught in the stranglehold of their liberators, the *nomenklatura* of Eastern Europe in general were unable to tolerate such authentic eyewitness accounts as this book" (212). The book has become a best seller; there are Dutch, French, German, Hebrew, Italian, Spanish, Swedish, and Japanese versions. Roman Polansky's film *The Pianist,* which appeared while I was still writing this book, has made Szpilman's story famous. Incidentally, I saw the film in Warsaw in September 2002 and discussed it with Alina Brodzka Wald and other survivors of wartime Warsaw. All agreed on the faithfulness of the screen interpretation of Szpilman's book, and above all on the authenticity of the general *atmosphere* of those terrible times in the ghetto re-created by Polansky.[16]

16. Perhaps the most accurate, and very favorable, appraisal of these qualities of the film can be found in a Polish review by Alina Margolis-Edelman (2003), the wife of Marek Edelman, the last commandant of the ghetto uprising.

In contrast, three other important diaries written in the ghetto were rapidly published because their publication took place far away from Communist control. The first is a journal written in Polish by a young Jewish girl, Mary Berg (also known as Miriam Wattenberg), the daughter of an American citizen. In January 1943 she was sent from the Warsaw ghetto (or more precisely, from Pawiak prison, where she was placed just before the "Resettlement") to a special camp in France. She was brought to Lisbon and on March 5, 1944, Mary and her mother were exchanged, together with other American and Allied citizens as well as wounded American prisoners of war, for German prisoners of war. An English translation of her intelligent and historically valuable testimony appeared in the United States in the last months of the war. Likewise, both Jonas Turkow's and Hillel Seidman's journals were promptly published outside devastated and controlled Poland.[17] Turkow was an outstanding director of Yiddish and Polish theater. His memoir is important for his description of theatrical activities and the history of the organized social services in the ghetto. Seidman's journal contains entries from July 12, 1942, to March 15, 1943, written from an Orthodox point of view. Neither Turkow nor Seidman was particularly interested in the presence of converts in the ghetto.

Recently, an important collection of eyewitness accounts, mostly fragments, taken from the ŻIH archives and edited by Michał Grynberg, were translated into English (Grynberg 1988, 2002). Two of them are pertinent for our purpose. All these accounts of life in the ghetto as well as of the vicissitudes of those who escaped on the "Other Side" are moving in their immediacy. The accounts are accompanied by careful notes.

There is no doubt in my mind that the omissions and errors in Sloan's version of Ringelblum's *Notes,* the unavailability of Hirszfeld's autobiography in English, and various delays in the translation or publication of other important documents have contributed in great part to the almost universal ignorance or misconceptions, particularly in Western Europe and in America, about the existence of Christian communities in the Warsaw ghetto. I believe that a documented history of the Christian communities inside the Warsaw ghetto could hardly have been written before the fall of Communism.

––––––

17. Turkow's *That's How It Was* was published in Yiddish in Buenos Aires in 1948. There are also Hebrew (1969) and French (1995) translations. Seidman's *Warsaw Ghetto Diary* was published in Yiddish in Buenos Aires in 1947. There is also a Hebrew (1957), an English (1997), and a French (1998) translation of this book.

Most of the available materials concerning Christians in the ghetto can be divided roughly into the following, not always mutually exclusive, categories:

1. German documents, including German newspapers in Polish such as *Gazeta Żydowska* and *Nowy Kurier Warszawski.*
2. Personal diaries and other documents written during the existence of the ghetto or very shortly after its destruction which have now been edited with adequate explanatory notes and comments.
3. Documents written during the existence of the ghetto but not yet edited and annotated.
4. Memoirs of survivors or bystanders written after the events described.
5. Critical commentaries on the above sources written by historians specializing in the period.

All five categories contain useful and important materials, but I wish to stress some works of a relatively recent date in the last category. English-speaking readers have at their disposal a good general history of the Warsaw ghetto written by Yisrael Gutman (1982). At the same time, an excellent social history concentrating on the detail of everyday life in the ghetto and stressing the diversity of that *Zwangsgesellschaft* is available only in Polish. I have in mind Ruta Sakowska's *People from the Closed District* (1993). This study is based on the author's doctoral dissertation, defended in the Institute of History of the Polish Academy of Sciences and entitled *"Social Life in the Warsaw Ghetto"* (*Życie społeczne w getcie warszawskim*), a title that perhaps better reflects the main thrust of Sakowska's study.

There are also some sophisticated investigations into the nature of those texts written in the atmosphere of the ghetto. In 1982 Roman Zimand attempted an appraisal of Czerniaków's *Diary*. In 1996 Barbara Engelking published a Polish work entitled *"Time has ceased to exist for me . . .": An Analysis of the Experience of Time in the Final Situation* which studied the writings of authors facing death. And in 1997 the literary scholar Jacek Leociak produced an exhaustive study, *The Text and the Shoah*. Although intended primarily as a literary analysis of the diverse writing coming out of the ghetto, Leociak's study is, to my mind, also a precious aid in understanding the specific historical context in which this extraordinary literature came to life. Furthermore, Leociak carefully provides explanatory notes, which must invariably accompany documents often written hastily and always bearing the mark of a cryptic, conspiratorial style. He also checks the sometimes scanty information about the authors, their circumstances and the reasons for their compositions. This enables him, for example, to present the most accurate appraisal of Hirszfeld's autobiography. Leociak's knowledge of the history of the ghetto texts, combined with his sophisticated interpretative abilities, makes his study indispensable to any serious investigation of the history of the Warsaw ghetto. More recently, in 2001, Engelking and Leociak published in Polish their important *The Warsaw Ghetto: Guide to to the Non-existing City.*

Permit me at this juncture to express a desideratum. I believe that it would be beneficial for sustaining the memories of the Shoah if such specific witnesses to the life and death of the Warsaw ghetto were translated into English. The most important Jewish witness of the Warsaw ghetto, Emanuel Ringelblum, should speak to the Western world in his own words and not in truncated and bowdlerized versions. A new and fully annotated translation of his *Togbukh* (1961) is the only way to restore to us the words of this great man. Ringelblum deserves a translation equal to the English version of Adam Czerniaków's *Warsaw Diary.*

But there are also other important works that have no English translations. I think particularly of Ludwik Hirszfeld's *Historia.* It is simply incomprehensible to me that such an important human and social document, authentically depicting the moral atmosphere of the war, animated by a truly extraordinary moral sense, and clearly written by a great scientist, has not been made available to the reading public outside Poland and Serbia. Marek Edelman, the last surviving commandant of the ghetto uprising, wrote his *Ghetto Fights* soon after the war. This priceless testimony to the events was published in English in London (1990) by a socialist press (Bookmarks). It is accompanied by a distinctly "sectarian" political introduction.[18] The book is currently out of print. A German translation from Polish appeared in 1993.

I also believe that the historians of the Shoah and their reading public would profit greatly from the availability in English of such detailed analyses of ghetto society as have now been published in Polish, after the demise of the Soviet-sponsored government. They present the complexity of the cultural and historical background. I have in mind such painstaking historians as Ruta Sakowska, especially her *People from the Closed District,* and such literary, historical, and sociological interpreters of wartime documents as Jacek Leociak and Barbara Engelking.

18. The book bears Edelman's disclaimer: "The introduction that follows refers to Leon Trotsky. I have never been a supporter of the ideas of Trotsky, which are foreign to me. . . . My agreement to the publication of this edition does not give exclusive rights to Bookmarks for future publications" (3).

CHAPTER THREE

A Brief History of the Warsaw Ghetto

To understand fully the Warsaw ghetto or any aspect of the Shoah, especially the gradual development of the machine of destruction, we first need an understanding of the chronology of events. The date of any journal entry is of crucial importance, because what the population of the ghetto knew and expected in February 1940 was one thing and something quite different a year later, and entirely different in April 1942. Ringelblum writing in February 1940 is, so to speak, a different person from Ringelblum of April 1942.

Schematically, the chronology of the Warsaw ghetto can be presented as four successive periods:

1. October 1939–November 1940: gradual isolation and gathering of the Jewish population.
2. November 1940–July 1942: the ghetto sealed off from the "Other Side."
3. July 22, 1942–September 15, 1942: the "Resettlement," which will also be referred to by its German euphemism, *Aktion*, that is, the transport to Treblinka and the liquidation of more than 300,000 Jews.
4. October 1942–May 1943: the "residual" ghetto (German: *Restghetto*), the Jewish resistance and uprising, followed by the total destruction of the ghetto. This last period, although crucial to the history of the Shoah in Warsaw, lies beyond the purview of this study.

Let us look more closely at the basic chronology. At the time of the German invasion of Poland, on September 1, 1939, there were 3.5 million Jews living in the country, chiefly in its central and eastern parts. Jews constituted a full 10 percent of the population and made up the largest Jewish community in Europe. The Jewish population of Warsaw, second largest after New York City, was more than 350,000, almost one-third of the city's total population. Legally, the Jews in Poland were treated as Poles of Mosaic confession (*Polacy wyznania mojżeszowego*), although the feeling that they belonged to a different nationality was common to both Jews and non-Jews. Certainly, the anti-Semites, who were growing in numbers and virulence in the second half of the 1930s, tended to consider the Jews as foreign nationals. Xenophobia and anti-Semitism went hand in hand.

The key to understanding the situation of the Jews before the war is their diversity. The Jews were divided along cultural, educational, economic, political, religious, and linguistic lines. These divisions are important to the study of the population of the Warsaw ghetto. Antony Polonsky sums up the situation of Polish Jewry in 1918–39:

> In the new Polish state, which inherited territory from Prussia, Russia, and Austria after World War I, regional differences developed in Jewish cultural and political patterns. But the general weakness of trends toward assimilation and integration persisted, as did the threefold division of political life into Zionist, Bundist and Orthodox camps. In spite of the economic and political difficulties that the community faced, particularly after the death of the Polish statesman Józef Piłsudski in 1935, it remained a vital source of Jewish secular and religious creativity in Yiddish, in Hebrew, and increasingly in Polish. (2001, 487)

Thus, unlike the situation in Western Europe, the majority of Polish Jews were not assimilated and they spoke Yiddish, sometimes exclusively. This was particularly true of Jews from the former Russian empire. To give an idea of the linguistic preferences among literate Jews in the middle of 1930, let us note that out of 204 specifically Jewish periodicals (with a total circulation of some 540,000) 75 percent were in Yiddish, 20 percent in Polish, and 5 percent in Hebrew.[1]

The war started on September 1, 1939. Jews lived in all parts of the city, but poor Jews tended to congregate in the northern part, which would soon

---

1. "Manual for the Rank and File Police" [in Polish], p. 12ss; typescript consulted in the New Acts Archives (Archiwum Akt Nowych) in Warsaw. I wish to thank the director, Dr. Tadeusz Krawczak, for his kind assistance in guiding me through the documents concerning the Jewish population of the ghetto.

be declared the Jewish living quarter (*Jüdisches Wohnbezirk*) by the Germans. On Rosh Hashanah, September 12 and 13, the neighborhood of Warsaw inhabited by numerous poor Jews was heavily bombed. The first step toward the creation of the ghetto was the posting of German signs at the boundaries of the quarter that read, "Closed Area of Epidemic. Through traffic only" (*Seuchensperrgebiet. Nur Durchfahrt gestattet*).

Beginning in October 1939, the western parts of Poland (Danzig, Pomerania, Silesia, and the Poznań and Łódź districts) were incorporated outright into the Reich (the Annexed Territories). The districts of Cracow, Radom, Warsaw, and Lublin were combined into the General Government (*Generalgouvernement*, or GG). (The name goes back to the German occupation of these territories during World War I.) The GG soon became the depository for the Polish and Jewish populations expelled from the Annexed Territories. The eastern parts of Poland, beyond the river Bug, were taken by the Soviet Union and incorporated into the Belorussian and the Ukrainian Soviet Republics.

In October 1939 the *Judenrat* was created with Adam Czerniaków as chairman (*Obmann*). By decree of General Governor Hans Frank, Jews were ordered to perform unpaid, obligatory labor. On October 29, 1939, the *Judenrat* began to conduct a census of the Jewish population of Warsaw at the request of the German authorities. The census, completed at the end of November, showed 359,827 Jews living in Warsaw. This number was growing rapidly, however, because in October–November 1939 Jews began to be expelled from the Annexed Territories and to arrive in Warsaw and in other future ghettos in the GG. At the same time, hundreds of thousands of Poles were also forced to resettle in the GG.

In November 30, 1939, the Polish-language German paper *Nowy Kurier Warszawski* announced that the governor of the Warsaw district, Ludwig Fischer, had ordered that as of December 1, 1939, all Jews twelve years and older had to wear a distinctive mark whenever they were outside their dwellings. The order also applied to the Jews coming from other districts and residing temporarily in Warsaw. Nonobservance of this decree would be severely punished. This distinctive mark was a white armband with a blue Star of David, to be worn on the right arm.

This was certainly the earliest but by no means the only decree of that kind issued by the Nazis. It coincides more or less with the order in the city of Łódź, in the Annexed Territories, that Jews wear first a yellow armband and later a yellow star on the upper right breast. These two decrees precede by some three months the decree forcing Poles to wear a distinctive mark while working in the territory of the Old Reich. This mark was a diamond shape five centimeters long bearing a violet letter *P* (for Pole) on a yellow background with violet borders. It too was to be worn on the upper right breast. This distinguishing mark (German: *Kennzeichen*) was made obligatory on March 8, 1940.

After the outbreak of the German-Soviet war, forced laborers from the territory of the Soviet Union were obliged to wear a similar sign, but with the letters *Ost* instead of *P.* Like the Star of David, the "petka" and the "ostka" carried with them many limitations of personal freedom and much outright discrimination. Noncompliance was punishable by fine, imprisonment, flogging, or a combination of the three (Seeber 1964, 154–56).

I remember well that the wearing of *P* in Germany was widely discussed among the non-Jewish and Jewish population of Warsaw at the beginning of the war. The introduction of the "petka" for Polish forced laborers in Germany, as well as many other measures taken by Germans at the beginning of the war, tended to diminish the sense that the Nazis' plans were specifically anti-Jewish.

The obligation to wear Star of David armbands in Warsaw (and in Łódź) preceded by about ten months a similar order for the Jews in the pre-1939 Reich and by about twenty-nine months one for the Jews in German-occupied France and Belgium. The order to wear the armband was also a first attempt and a provisional step in defining a "Jew" in the GG.

The December 1, 1939, decree considered as a Jew (1) anyone who belonged or had belonged to the Jewish confessional community; (2) anyone whose father or mother belonged or had belonged to the Jewish confessional community. In order to understand the confusion of such a "definition," we must understand the gist of Polish laws before 1939. Every citizen was defined by his membership in a confessional community (*grupa wyznaniowa*)— Jewish, Catholic, Protestant, or Greek Orthodox. In practice, it was nearly impossible to declare oneself to be without religion, and as Ruta Sakowska points out, such declarations were extremely rare. Between 1926 and 1930 only seventy-eight voting-age males in Warsaw made a declaration of "confessionlessness" (*bezwyznaniowość*) (Sakowska 1993, 13). Those who declared themselves in this way risked real difficulties in registering and in obtaining birth, marriage, and death certificates, because the whole system of civil registry was based on the confessional communities.

The December 1 decree fundamentally changed the Polish legal definition for "Jewishness" because it now included those who had formerly belonged to the Jewish confessional community and those whose parents had belonged to it. This definition encompassed first- and second-generation baptized Jews. It was not surprising that many known neophytes declared themselves Jewish by wearing the Star of David. But many of them did not. The Landy family, for example, decided not to declare themselves Jewish; neither the Christians among them nor the atheists (or confessionless) declared that their parents had been members of the Jewish confessional community. In general, those with strong connections to the political left did not accept the Star of David armbands because they had far fewer illusions about the Nazis' intentions. They also reacted more emotionally than others against the systematic destruction of those "lives unworthy of living."

Before going any further with the historical account, we must touch briefly on the administrative arrangements set up by the occupiers. Though they did not allow any forms of Polish (puppet) government, the Germans retained a minimal Polish city administration. The president of the City Council, Stefan Starzyński, the moving spirit of the defense of Warsaw in September 1939, was arrested by the Gestapo immediately after the city's capitulation. He died in the Nazi concentration camp Baelberge in 1944. Julian Kulski, the vice president of the City Council, was named commissar-president of Warsaw and worked under the German administration. In this function, he collaborated with the *Judenrat* and met with Czerniaków. After the war, he wrote "Recollections of Czerniaków" (Kulski 1972). Unlike Czerniaków, who was criticized by the partisans of resistance, Kulski and his activities were tacitly supported both by the Polish government-in-exile and by the underground authorities, and there was no controversy after the war concerning either him or his role under the occupation.

More important for the Polish population was the Polish Main Welfare Council (Rada Główna Opiekuńcza, or RGO). The RGO, designed after its prototype during the German occupation of 1916–18, was created to let the Poles take care of the refugees and orphans. The RGO was established partly because American charitable organizations, acting in Poland in 1939–41, insisted that their aid must not be administered by the Germans. Adam Ronikier, chairman during the greater part of the occupation, collaborated secretly with the Catholic bishops of the GG, with the Jewish Mutual Aid Committee (Żydowska Samopomoc Społeczna, or ŻSS), and later with the underground group Żegota. In some ways, his situation resembled Czerniaków's. He tried to navigate between the German might and terror, his conscience, and the increasing control and pressure of the underground. According to Andrzej Pankowicz, "Ronikier intervened on behalf of the Jews several times between January 1941 and July 1942. He demanded that the Germans stop constructing ghettos and stop deportations. In 1942, he was interrogated by the Gestapo for his defense of Christian-Jews. He protested against the use of Polish peasants and Polish *Baudienst* [the obligatory Construction Service] in the obligatory auxiliary work in Treblinka. After the disbanding of the Jewish Mutual Aid Committee, he hid Michał Weichert, the last president of the ŻSS, in his own apartment" (1989, 20). (Weichert, by the way, survived the war and died in Israel.) In October 1943, Ronikier was dismissed from his job by the Germans, but he maintained close contact with the RGO. When he learned that the Soviet authorities had accused him of "collaboration," he fled to the West at the end of the war. He died in the United States in 1952.

Ronikier, the only representative of any Polish "authority" recognized by the Germans, was asked to interpret the December 1 decree. Some prominent members of Polish society, such as Ludwik Hirszfeld, found the decree ambiguous because for many years they had not had any sense of belonging to the Jewish community and did belong to the Christian confessional community. They asked Ronikier to clarify with the German authorities the legal status of the Jewish Christians. The Germans pretended to listen to Ronikier's inquires, told him that they would look into the matter, and asked for the list of interested persons. The Christian Jews on this list did not wear the armbands until February 1941, when they were arrested and expelled to the ghetto. Hirszfeld, as we shall see, describes the situation of the "Ronikiers" (*Ronikierzy*), as they would be called by the ghetto population.

Hirszfeld believed that the RGO had furnished the list of the "Ronikiers" to the German authorities. It is most unlikely, however, that Ronikier, or one of his close collaborators, would have furnished the Germans with the list of the "special" Christian Jews. They were past masters in deferring such actions while dealing with German orders. Instead, this was probably the work of a Gestapo informer inside the RGO Warsaw branch. In March 2001, during my research in the Polish New Acts Archives in Warsaw, I found the following statement: "Stefan Idzikowski a. k. Idźkowski, of Jewish origin, an employee of the Warsaw Branch of the RGO, is alleged [*jest poszlakowany*] to have handed over to the Germans the list of the baptized Jews who remained in the Aryan district of Warsaw. Signed 'Lilka,' on April 25, 1941 (K-C no. 30 169)."[2] This matter, like many others of that nature, was never cleared up.

The decree of December 1, 1939, thus brought the definition of "Jewishness" to the forefront. But the German determination of who was a Jew

---

2. MF 2225/6 "Reports from the Ghetto to the Delegate of the Polish Government-in-Exile."

showed itself far more clearly in the so-called Kott affair. If there were any hopes that the Germans would consider converts or the descendants of converts as non-Jews, they should have evaporated in January 1940, when the Kott affair took place. Yisrael Gutman describes the events:

> A poster was issued bearing the photograph of a young man stating that "the Jew Andrzej Kott" was wanted for suspicion of murder and whoever turned him in would receive 2,000 zlotys. Kott, the son of converts . . . was among the founders of the underground movement PLAN, which was made up mostly of the young members of the Polish intelligentsia and aspired to reconstitute an independent Polish State committed to principles of social justice. Kott was the head of the "Fighting Division" of this underground organization and obviously had no connection whatsoever with Jews and Jewish affairs. After the movement's first few actions, the most prominent of its members, including Kott, were caught. But Kott succeeded in escaping, and this drove the Nazis wild. (1982, 33–34)[3]

They went wild, because Kott's was the first (and last) successful escape from Gestapo headquarters. Their rage turned against Jews: 255 Jewish hostages were taken; all were ultimately killed. This affair is mentioned in many of the ghetto diaries. Ringelblum notes the Kott affair under February 21, 1940: "Rumor that Kott broadcast from France" (1988, 95). Sloan wrongly identifies "Kot" as a "Leader of the Polish Peasant Party" (Ringelblum 1958, 21). Ringelblum also gives a short account of the Kott affair to commemorate his friend Szymon Lubelski, who died as one of the Jewish hostages, in the appendix to his *Kronika,* written in 1943 and entitled "Silhouettes" (*Sylwetki*) (the "Silhouettes" are not part of Sloan's version). Ringelblum does not mention Kott's religion, probably because he knew that it was generally known. He also repeats the false information that Kott broadcast from London. Kaplan, too, explains the affair: "[Kott] did whatever he did, and fled, and here the conquerors found an open field for revenge against their forfeit people. Kot's [*sic*] grandmother was a Jew three generations back and the whole Jewish people must bear the sin of her Jewishness" (1999, 106).

---

3. Gutman bases his account on the article by Rutkowski (1967). Rutkowski adds two details: Kott, who is sometimes referred to as Kazimierz, was in fact called Kazimierz Andrzej Kott. This twenty-year-old patriot was hiding in Warsaw. Later he escaped to the Soviet part of Poland and was deported to the USSR, where he died sometime during the war (66 n. 14).

I remember well the German poster and the reactions of Christian Jews to Kott's being considered a Jew. That poster and the taking of the hostages told more about the "Nuremberg Law" mentality of the new rulers of Warsaw than any oral announcement or written decree.

In January 1940 the Germans ordered the closing of all Jewish houses of prayer—but not the churches—in the territory of the future ghetto and elsewhere in Warsaw. The order prohibited meetings of *minyanim* in private dwellings. This order was supposedly based on the danger of typhus. Needless to say, it was observed in the breach.

That same month the Germans introduced food ration cards, which soon would entitle the Jews to lower rations than the Poles. It was one of the Germans' attempts to create a chasm between the Jewish and the Polish populations. During and after Holy Week of 1940, a mob of young Polish hoodlums—if not incited, certainly tolerated by the Germans—robbed Jewish stores and attacked many of the Jews, chiefly in the Jewish quarter. Such activities took place sporadically throughout 1940.

Considering the situation in Warsaw at the beginning of 1940 from a Jewish point of view, it is difficult to think that the Jews were the *only* real or intended victims of the Germans. The large-scale expulsions from the Annexed Territories to the GG, often carried out in a barbarous manner, were affecting both Jews and non-Jews—that is, all Jews and all "nationally conscious" Poles were subject to expulsions.

Furthermore, in the spring of 1940 the Germans rounded up thousands of "Aryans," but not Jews, for forced labor in Germany. Ringelblum reports on May 8, 1940: "Horrifying day. At twilight, Poles were seized in every street. Jews had their papers checked to make sure that they weren't Christians. Stopped streetcars, dragged everyone in them off to the Pawia Street prison; from there, it is said they are sent to Prussia" (1958, 38). At the same time, the chairman of the *Judenrat* notes with irony: "Some Poles are beginning to wear Jewish armbands [to avoid being taken for labor in Germany]. Somebody started a rumor that we have made special representation to the Germans, lest, God forbid, our bands were taken away" (Czerniaków 1999, 147). Such "confusing" reactions to the persecutions of the "Aryans" appear in the journals even after the ghetto was sealed off. Ten months later, in reprisal for the execution of a *Volksdeutsch* director of a theater, a Gestapo collaborator, by the Polish underground, the Germans began a series of repressions of the Poles. Kaplan comments on the events of March 9, 1941, and on the reactions inside the ghetto:

The people of the ghetto are happy and sad at the same time. They are happy that the Lord created a ghetto for them, for if it weren't for the ghetto, we and the Poles would be in the same trouble, and they are sad that the conquerors lengthened the curfew for the Gentiles, which means a lessening of chance for smuggling.

In time of disaster a great panic hits the Gentiles and they begin to huddle close to us. This time too, many Poles escaped secretly and illegally from the Aryan quarter and came to live for awhile in the Jewish ghetto. They even wrapped the "badge of shame" on their right arms to disguise their origin. (254)

Until the sealing off of the ghetto, these specifically anti-Polish measures tended to postpone the realization that the Jews were in fact the primary object of the occupier's wrath. I have not found anywhere in the wartime literature the opinion that the fact that Jews were not sent to Germany to become "free" slave workers, that is to say, to work outside the camps, boded ill for the future of the Warsaw Jewish community.

To return to the chronology: In April 1940 construction began on the walls. The area inside those walls was labeled "Closed Area of Epidemic" (*Seuchensperrgebiet*) and would later become the ghetto. Throughout the summer and autumn of 1940, the Jews, still free to move in the city, were subject to constant restrictions, robberies, beatings, and regulations and chicaneries such as forbidden areas, special streetcars for Jews only, curfew in the *Seuchesperrgebiet* from 7 p.m. to 8 a.m., and so on.

On May 29, 1940, the *Judenrat* created the Jewish Mutual Aid Committee (Żydowska Samopomoc Społeczna, or ŻSS). All Jewish welfare and charity institutions became part of the ŻSS. Here again the Germans wished to give the impression that they were creating a "self-governing" district, a sort of mirror image of the Polish quarter. The ŻSS became a sort of Jewish RGO.

On October 2, 1940, the German authorities officially established not only the Jewish district but also, typically, the Polish and the German living quarters in Warsaw. The exact boundaries of the Jewish quarter were established. Within three weeks some 115,000 "Aryans" were forced to leave the Jewish district and some 140,000 Jews were crowded into what became de facto the ghetto. It is important to note that although the word "ghetto" began to be used regularly at this time, it never had any official standing; in fact, the use of the term was forbidden by the Nazis (Ringelblum 1958, 85).

Most writers used the terms "closed quarter" (*zamknięta dzielnica*), or simply "quarter" (*dzielnica*).

The walls constructed around the Jewish quarter were more than ten feet high with additional barbed wire on top. The exits into the "Aryan" side were controlled by the German police (*Schutzpolizei* or *Ordnungspolizei*), the Polish police (called the "blue police"), and the newly formed Jewish Order Service.

The turning point came on November 15, 1940. The Jewish residential quarter, which had been diminished to about two-thirds of its former size, was sealed off. The walls previously surrounding the *Seuchensperrgebiet* were replaced by new walls built to the new dimensions of the ghetto; these became known as "the Wall." Inhabitants now required a special pass to leave and enter the ghetto. A blue policeman stationed in the car guarded the car entrance. Streetcars were allowed to cross the district, but not to stop. It was on such a streetcar that I saw the crowded ghetto and the sick and dying lying on the streets, when, virtually every day, I rode the no. 17 on Bonifraterska Street.

The newly established ghetto, whose frontiers were to gradually shrink, contained about 350,000 persons; constant waves of resettled Jews from parts of the Warsaw district and, later, from other parts of the GG and Germany would add to this number. As a well-informed editor of a ghetto diarist observed: "In Warsaw, as elsewhere, the Germans also put Gypsies into the ghetto. They wore white armbands bearing the letter Z (for *Zigeuner*). They quickly disappeared from the ghetto, apparently having managed to escape" (Lewin 1988, 250 n. 72).[4] We know that later the Germans sent Gypsies directly to the concentration and annihilation camps.

Living conditions in the ghetto were quite bad before the sealing off and deteriorated very quickly. Most of the working population was prevented from making a living. Overcrowding, lack of food, lack of basic hygienic conditions, all took an awesome toll in this the largest of all the ghettos. The poor Jews living in the quarter before it became the ghetto and, above all, the poor newcomers from surrounding towns were the first victims of disease and starvation. The contrast between the rich and the poor, and the growing indifference toward the sick and dying, would become constant themes in the diaries of ghetto dwellers.

---

4. Hilberg estimates that "between April and June 1942 nearly a thousand Gypsies from the Warsaw district . . . [and] Hamburg were sent to the Warsaw ghetto. They were swept up in the deportation of the Jews" (2001, 276).

In closing the ghetto, the occupier meant to create both a temporary isolation area—supposedly for hygienic reasons—and a camp for compulsory labor with its own work centers. Early in 1941, the Germans created several workshops and manufacturing plants owned by various German firms and producing various goods for the needs and profit of the Germans.

In April 1941 the German authorities, stressing that the Jewish quarter was "self-governed," allowed the opening of theaters performing in Yiddish and Polish. At the same time, they lifted the ban imposed in January 1940, on Jewish religious services in synagogues and in private dwellings. The Great Synagogue on Tłomackie Street was reopened in June 1941 with an imposing ceremony, only to be excluded from the ghetto territory in March 1942, and to be totally destroyed on May 16, 1943, to mark the German victory over the Jewish uprising in the ghetto.

Germany began the war against the Soviet Union on June 22, 1941. Shortly afterward, the Polish underground press began to print terrible news from the East. There were mass killings by the *Einsatzgruppen* operating behind German lines, mass executions in the towns of Białystok, Vilna, Lwów (Lvov), in the Tarnopol and Stanisławów districts as well as in Lithuania. The educated class in the ghetto received this news, either directly from the underground Polish press or from conversations with people on the "Aryan" side. It must be remembered that telephone and postal services into and out of the ghetto were functioning even after the *Aktion*. Many letters sent to the ghetto from the outside gave veiled information about the destruction of Jews.[5]

But news received toward the end of 1941 that the Germans had opened a concentration camp in Chełmno nad Nerem (Kulmhof) to which Jews from the small towns in the Annexed Territories were routinely being sent to be killed was not readily believed by the Jewish population at large. Immediately after the war, Marek Edelman, the second in command in the Jewish uprising and one of the two commanders of the ŻOB who survived, spoke about this disbelief: "The Warsaw ghetto did not believe the news. All the people clinging desperately to life could not accept the fact that this life could be taken from them from them in this way. Only the politically organized youth observing the gradual growth of German terror accepted this news as likely or

5. Some of them found their way to the Ringelblum Archives and were recently published; see Sakowska (1997, e.g., letter #37); also, Sakowska (1963).

true. They decided to begin a large action spreading the news to convince the society of it" (1993, 125). By "politically organized youth," Edelman meant those belonging to the socialist Bund. The idea that "the ghetto does not believe" is reiterated throughout Edelman's report. Edelman's significant testimony was written immediately after the war and was published in Polish by the Central Committee of the Bund in Warsaw in 1945. In 1983 it was reprinted both clandestinely in Poland and in Paris (in French) by the Polish Literary Institute. Later it was republished in Poland. As I have already mentioned, this important memoir, written by the last surviving commandant of the ghetto fighters, appeared in English in 1990. I hope that it will be republished in a fully annotated version.[6]

The Nazis coupled the terror with various attempts to hide their true intentions. Thus on October 1, 1941, the Germans, trying to instill a sense of "normal" life in the ghetto, permitted the opening of six primary schools which would operate until June 1942. Before and after this permission, many clandestine teaching activities on all levels of education were conducted in the ghetto.

On October 15, 1941, the German authorities published a decree reiterating a similar decree promulgated in January 1941 which specified a death sentence for all Jews who left the ghetto without official authorization. The death penalty was also officially imposed on any person sheltering or offering help to Jews outside the ghetto. It is important to stress that any assistance given to Jews was punishable by death only in Poland and in the Soviet territories occupied by the German army.

During the second half of 1941 and the first half of 1942 the continued reduction in the size of the ghetto caused increased crowding, hunger, and poverty. The most graphic description of the deadly conditions of the poor, homeless, and starving masses in the ghetto before the *Aktion* is to be found in Edelman (1993, 120–24). The "natural" death rate from malnutrition, typhus, and tuberculosis was more than made up for by forcing into the ghetto Jews from smaller towns in the Warsaw district, as well as Gypsies and some German Jews.

The end of the second stage of the ghetto destruction came in July 1942, when the *Aktion,* or the deportations to the Treblinka extermination camp, began. The *Aktion* was preceded by selective arrests and executions of prominent and socially active persons. Fifty-two were shot on the night of

6. The most readily available text in English which contains some of Edelman's views is Krall (1977).

April 17/18 and many more in the period until July 22. The aim was to terrorize the population and to stifle any resistance to the imminent deportations.

These deportations started on the morning of July 22. The German police, the Polish police, and the Ukrainian, Latvian, and Lithuanian auxiliaries were posted along the Wall, outside the ghetto. The officers of the newly created Resettlement Staff (*Umsiedlungsstab*) announced to the *Judenrat* that all the nonproductive Jews would be resettled to work in the East.

On the second day of *Aktion,* the head of the *Judenrat,* Adam Czerniaków, helpless in the face of deportations and unwilling to collaborate in their organization, committed suicide by taking poison. Yisrael Gutman describes reactions to his death:

> [His] suicide had repercussions throughout the ghetto and was interpreted in various ways. Those close to Czerniakow, who valued his efforts as the chairman of the *Judenrat,* believed that his final act was a testimony to his personal courage and sense of public responsibility. Others—and particularly circles in the underground who resolutely denounced the policy of the *Judenrat*—claimed that Czerniakow's act of self-destruction at the time of a supreme trial was evidence of his weakness, and some charged that he had not even summoned up the courage to warn the ghetto before taking his own life or at least warn his close associates and issue a call for resistance. (1982, 206–7)

As we have seen, the controversy caused by Czerniaków's suicide lasted long into the postwar period, and was further complicated by Soviet ideas about collaboration with the Germans.

Although Czerniaków knew that the *Aktion* meant destruction, the majority of the ghetto population did not realize the final outcome of the deportations. A report entitled "Liquidation of the Jewish Warsaw," dated November 15, 1942, was prepared by the United Jewish Underground Organizations for the Polish government-in-exile and for the Allied governments. The report insists that both before and during the *Aktion* the population of the ghetto thought that deportation (*Umsiedlung*) was nothing more than transportation to another ghetto or to another workplace. The members of the *Judenrat,* who had received the most solemn assurances about the safety of the deported, did not believe the news coming from the "Aryan" side about the liquidation of the Jews (Sakowska 1980, 279 and passim).

After Czerniaków's death, his second in command, Marek Lichtenbaum, became the head of the *Judenrat,* but the *Judenrat* would now be much diminished. Henceforth, the Germans relied directly on the Jewish Order Service, which played an important role in the *Aktion.* Its commandant, Józef Szeryński, a neophyte and a prewar inspector in the Polish police, was arrested by the Gestapo on May 1, 1942, for illegal commerce in furs between the ghetto and the "Aryan" side. He was released briefly before the *Aktion.* His replacement, Jakub Lejkin, played a diligent role in rounding up people for deportation. In fact, in his entry for December 12, 1942, Ringelblum states that "Lejkin, the chief of police, bears the main guilt for the Resettlement" (1988a, 429); "[Lejkin was] in charge of the resettlement" (Ringelblum 1958, 333). Szeryński was the object of an assassination attempt by the Jewish underground. Wounded in the face on August 20, 1942, he committed suicide sometime in January 1943. Ludwik Hirszfeld gives quite a negative picture of Szeryński: "He could have died directing a military unit and his name would have been pronounced with reverence by his friends and by his enemies. He was not big enough for it, and so he died like Judas. At the end of the *Aktion,* he was wounded by a bullet fired by a member of his own tribe [*współplemieniec*], and later apparently he took his own life" (2000, 390). Ringelblum, always critical of the *Judenrat* and the Jewish Order Service, writes on December 5, 1942: "The Jewish Police had a very bad name even before the resettlement. The Polish Police didn't take part in the forced-work press gangs, but the Jewish police engaged in that ugly business. Jewish policemen also distinguished themselves with fearful corruption and immorality. But they reached the height of viciousness during the resettlement" (1958, 329).

The *Aktion* lasted until Yom Kippur, September 21, 1942. More than 300,000 persons were moved to the *Umschlagplatz* (lit. "transfer place") and from there to the extermination camp of Treblinka.[7] The last deportation included the members of the Jewish Order Service and their families. Only 380 policemen were needed in the vastly reduced ghetto. At the end of the *Aktion* about 35,000 Jews belonging to the various workshops and to the skeleton *Judenrat* organization were allowed to remain in what the Germans called the residual ghetto (*Restghetto*). In addition, about 20,000 Jews without work papers were in hiding there.

---

7. The *Aktion* is described in detail in Gutman (1982, 197–227); see esp. 209–11, where the author discusses its four phases.

For all practical purposes, the *Aktion* ends the known history of Christian communities within the ghetto. The Jewish Christians who did not find shelter on the "Aryan" side perished with the Jews in Treblinka. The rest of the history of the ghetto in Warsaw, particularly its resistance, culminating in the armed struggle against Nazi forces by the ŻOB, the Jewish Fighting Organization (Żydowska Organizacja Bojowa) and by the ŻZW, Żydowski Jewish Military Union (Związek Wojskowy) between April 19 and May 8, 1943, is well known. But it is not a part of the Jewish Christian history of the ghetto. While there might have been some baptized Jews among the ghetto fighters, nothing is known about those individuals. The Jewish Christian community of the Warsaw ghetto ceased to exist in the early stages of the *Aktion*.

CHAPTER FOUR

Churches in the Ghetto and Their Parishioners

Before the war, there was no specific Jewish district in Warsaw. Jews lived in all districts, but there was a higher concentration of poor Jews in the northern part of what would be called in the United States the downtown area. Thus the Germans created the Jewish living quarter in that area, where up to 40 percent of the population consisted of non-Jews. When the Jewish living quarter became the ghetto, it contained three Roman Catholic parishes within its boundaries: Saint Augustine, the Nativity of the Blessed Virgin Mary (henceforth B.V.M.), and All Saints. The Church of the Nativity of the B.V.M. has been sometimes refered to by its former name of "the Carmelite church." We do not know of any Protestant or Greek Orthodox places of formal worship in the ghetto.

There was a Reformed-Evangelical church next to the Nativity of the B.V.M., but it was placed just outside the Wall, as an enclave in the ghetto territory. The Leszno Street entrance was walled up, and a special "corridor" into the church was made on the eastern side through a house on Przejazd Street. This "corridor" also allowed access to the Protestant Charles and Mary Hospital (Szpital Karola i Marii) which functioned just inside the ghetto until the *Aktion*. According to Iwona Stefańczyk, the Protestant Church, surrounded on three sides by the ghetto walls, "carried out significant charitable activities. In its territory some well-known escapes from the ghetto took place—people were jumping from the top of the Wall onto the church ground" (1997, 29).

Before the ghetto was sealed off, all three Roman Catholic parish churches served as regular places of Catholic worship, for both the "Aryan" and "non-Aryan" Christians. In Saint Augustine Church on Nowolipki Street, the nominal pastor was Rev. Karol Niemira, auxiliary bishop of Pińsk. After

1939, he was appointed to the head of the parish. His second in command and acting head was Rev. Franciszek Garncarek, who followed church laws requiring the pastor to remain with the church as long as he could. The other assistants were Rev. Zygmunt Kowalski and Rev. Leon Więckowicz. A postwar copy of the regularly kept church register in my possession bears the following marginal note, obviously written after the war: "Sometime after the sealing off of the ghetto, the church functioned as a place of worship for the Catholics of Jewish origin who lived in the ghetto. There were about five thousand of them. The priests lived outside the ghetto and commuted to the church with permanent passes. After some time, however, they were forbidden to enter and the services in the church ceased. This is according to the statement made by Rev. Zygmunt Kowalski, then the assistant in the Saint Augustine parish." In July 1941, after the church was deactivated, a well-known Jewish-Christian director, Marek Arensztajn, acting in Polish and Yiddish under the name of Andrzej Marek, organized a theater in the church hall. He was baptized in the ghetto. After the *Aktion*, the Germans turned the church into a furniture warehouse.

We know that Rev. Garncarek and his assistant were active in providing all sorts of help to the ghetto dwellers, but we do not have any details concerning this help. We know that Janusz Korczak (pseudonym of Dr. Henryk Goldszmit), the director of a large orphanage next to Saint Augustine Church, a renowned educator, physician, and writer, addressed a letter to Rev. Garncarek in February 1942: "[Since] Providence has thrust upon you a missionary role, I urge you to attend a meeting of the personnel of our orphanage to discuss ways of saving the lives of the children from destruction. [You could] perhaps offer some good advice, perhaps an ardent prayer" (Aleksander Lewin 1992, 129–30). We do not possess the text of the letter, but the notes on its contents were written by Dr. Korczak himself. We also know that Dr. Korczak maintained a friendly relationship with the priests of All Saints as well. Two priests of Saint Augustine Church did not survive the war. Rev. Garncarek died on December 20, 1943, outside the ghetto; he was shot on the steps of the presbytery of another church. His assistant, Rev. Więckowicz, was arrested for helping Jews on December 3, 1942, and died in the Gross-Rosen concentration camp on August 4, 1944 (see Engelking and Leociak 2001, 621).

The two other parishes, the Nativity of the B.V.M. on Leszno Street (now Solidarność Street) and All Saints on Grzybowski Square, were functioning places of Catholic worship until the first days of the *Aktion*. The Nativity Church was in the middle of the ghetto and the All Saints Church in the southeast corner. The church on Leszno was mentioned often by the

Jewish diarists of the ghetto, probably because it was more or less in the center of the closed quarter. All Saints, on the other hand, was mentioned more often by the Christians, because many of them lived in the vicinity.

A legend arose about the identity of the pastor of the Nativity Church. Ringelblum repeats this legend, noting on December 24 and 25, 1941, that "in the church on Leszno Street [the Nativity] there is a neophyte priest, [Tadeusz] Puder. It is well known that before the war he was struck on the face [by a member] of the ONR. Observers tell us that a great crowd of simple people, porters and such, come to the church on Leszno Street. Numerous Jewish see to it that they are not molested" (1988a, 342; missing in Ringelblum 1958). This incorrect information concerning the pastor was repeated by most Jewish and Polish writers until a recent study (Engelking and Leociak 2001, 621–22) discovered the error. Rev. Puder was a priest in Warsaw who had been stuck in the face, but he was not at Nativity Church and not in the ghetto. The wide acceptance of the error can probably be traced back to the passage in Ringelblum and his authoritative text. The presence of Rev. Puder in the ghetto must have been widely believed at the time, because Mary Berg also mentions it: "Only the Leszno Street church is open; regular services are held there, and the priests [sic] too, are of Jewish origin" (1945, 119). One reason for the legend may be that before the war Rev. Puder was involved in pastoral activities designed specifically for converts.

Indeed, Rev. Tadeusz Puder (1908–45) was a popular priest in Warsaw. He was a relative of the well-known writer and convert Leo Belmont (Leopold Blumental), who died in the ghetto and was buried in the Reformed-Evangelical cemetery. Rev. Puder was rector of the Church of Saint Hyacinth, remembered by many (including myself) because of the outrage of which he was a victim on July 3, 1938. While in liturgical vestments and going from the altar to the pulpit to preach, an assailant shouting "Jew!" struck him in the face. The assailant, Rafał Michalski, was a follower of the Radical National Camp (Obóz Narodowo Radykalny, or ONR). The cries of horror caused by this sacrilegious act ceased only when Rev. Puder proceeded with his prepared sermon (Heller 1980, 134).

Since Rev. Tadeusz Puder was active in the neophyte circles, his history should figure in a work treating Jewish Christians in Warsaw. The following facts concerning the priest were garnered from his "Personal File," reconstructed after the war, in the Archdiocesan Archives in Warsaw. Both of Rev. Puder's parents were of Jewish origin, but his mother was a deeply devout Christian. She waited until the death of her husband to be baptized. The fourteen-year-old Tadeusz and his two brothers were baptized with her.

Tadeusz was very pious and wished to become a priest. He entered the seminary in 1928 and studied in Rome, where he was elevated to the priesthood in 1932. He continued his theological studies there and in Jerusalem until 1937. A Bible specialist, Rev. Puder was closely associated with the Laski convent and Laski spirit.

On November 21, 1939, the administrator of the Warsaw diocese, Stanisław Gall, knowing that Rev. Puder's reputation and his "Jewish looks" would make his position in the parish dangerous, appointed him as a chaplain at a convent near Warsaw. The nuns of the Franciscan Sisters of the Family of Mary were soon to become very active in rescuing Jewish children, and Rev. Puder too was active in this work. As a result of a denunciation, he was arrested by the Gestapo on April 24, 1941. For unknown reasons the Germans did not send him to the ghetto. After being interrogated at the Gestapo headquarters, he was transferred to the Warsaw Mokotów prison, where the sisters managed to have him placed in a hospital. On November 7, 1942, he escaped, sliding down a rope made out of bed sheets into a waiting horse-drawn wagon. He hid under the coal and, later, dressed as a nun with a heavily bandaged head, came back to his mother's home. After a while, he again took up his position in the convent. The convent and the orphans were moved to another institution in the eastern part of the GG. Rev. Puder traveled dressed in a nun's habit. The Soviet Army liberated the town on September 18, 1944. On January 23, 1945, walking on a street of destroyed Warsaw, he was hit by a Soviet truck and died four days later from a head injury. For many years the accident was considered a planned assassination by the Soviet secret police, but there is no evidence that this is true.

The ONR, a political movement founded in 1934, figures prominently in the literature concerning the Shoah in Poland. It was a para-fascist, anti-Semitic organization that accepted many of the Nazi racist tenets. The ONR, like the Communist Party, was outlawed in Poland from its inception. Because of its professed program and its instigations of anti-Jewish excesses, the ONR represented the most extreme and vicious wing of anti-Semitism in Poland. During the war it was active in the underground. Its armed organization, the National Armed Forces (Narodowe Siły Zbrojne), was fighting the Germans but was alleged to have attacked the Jewish and Communist partisans.

If the Germans considered the Nazilike parties in Eastern Europe—like the Iron Guard in Romania or the Arrow Cross in Hungary—allies, they considered ONR an enemy, and rightly so, because the ONR was staunchly anti-German. More important, however, the Germans never intended any Polish pro-German government that would require allies.

Throughout the existence of the ghetto, the curate of the Nativity of the B.V.M. Church was Monsignor Seweryn Popławski, who was assisted by Rev. Henryk Komorowski, Rev. Teofil Głowacki, and Rev. Zyberk-Plater. Rev. Popłowski remained at his post even after the *Aktion*. Rev. Komorowski would be remembered as a charismatic, well-loved priest. He was in charge of the young people of the parish. From the fall of 1942 until the spring of 1943, when the church was on the southern tip of the residual ghetto, many people used its large basement as an escape route to the partly destroyed parts of the former ghetto (Pankiewicz 1997, 77).

The Church of All Saints on Grzybowski Square was built in 1867. Damaged by bombs in 1939, and almost totally destroyed in 1942 and in 1944, it was rebuilt after the war and is still the largest church building in Warsaw. It is perhaps interesting to note that the original architect of All Saints was Henryk Marconi, whose son Leandro was the chief designer of the Great Synagogue on nearby Tłomackie Street. The same neoclassical "gigantic" style characterizes both buildings. There is perhaps a symbolic significance in the fact that two communities, so far apart in so many ways, had this in common.

The pastor at All Saints was Monsignor Marceli Godlewski. His assistant and second in command was Rev. Antoni Czarnecki. Rev. Tadeusz Nowotko also served in the parish. Rev. Godlewski lived outside the ghetto and came to his parish every day; Rev. Czarnecki lived permanently in the rectory of the church. He left a brief memorandum, "The All Saints Parish" ("Parafia Wszystkich Świętych") written in 1973. Obviously conscious that he was writing under an unfriendly political regime, he prudently cites published sources and concentrates on the pastoral aspect of his work. Rev. Czarnecki's caution was fully justified. Rev. Godlewski's successor at All Saints, Rev. Zygmunt Kaczyński, was arrested in 1949 and received a ten-year sentence for "political crimes." He was murdered in prison in 1953, and rehabilitated by the Communist regime in 1958. Despite its caution, Rev. Czarnecki's article is important for many details. He mentions the visits of Dr. Janusz Korczak and his orphans to the church grounds. He also writes briefly about baptisms in the ghetto and the reasons for them. His opinions here are quite realistic: "It is difficult to ascertain now how much these catechumens were inclined to embrace the teaching of Christ because of their desire for faith and their supernatural intention, or how much they were motivated by a secret hope that the Christian confession figuring in their identity card could save them from destruction in that inhuman epoch" (Smólski 1981, 208–9). After having served as pastor at Saint Catherine Church in Warsaw, Rev. Czarnecki died in 1989.

Rev. Godlewski was doubtless a key figure among the Christians in the ghetto. During the time of his ghetto activities, he was already an old man, having been born in 1865. He became a priest in 1888 and studied in Rome at the Gregorian University. As a doctor of theology he continued his parish work, usually in humble parishes. Later he was a professor in the Warsaw Seminary. In 1905 he traveled to Belgium and Germany, where he became acquainted with the Catholic Worker Movement.

The All Saints parish was situated in a heavily Jewish neighborhood. Well before the war, Rev. Godlewski organized the housemaids in his parish and elsewhere, seeing to it that their employers, who were often Jews, paid the health insurance rates. He also organized the local artisans, who were often in conflict with the more numerous Jewish artisans. He was active in journalism and in Christian labor organizations. He founded an interest-free loan association, apparently using the Jewish Interest-Free Loan Association, as a model; he took its constitution and substituted the word "Jews" with "Poles." He was a nationalist and an "Endek," a member of the National Democratic Party (Stronnictwo Narodowo Demokratyczne, or ND).

In Godlewski's activities, he often came into conflict with local Jews and Jewish organizations and as a result acquired a reputation as an anti-Semite. It is important to note that this idea of anti-Semitism was based on the economic competition between the Yiddish-speaking "foreigners" and the "real" Poles. Right-wing parties, such as the ND, took advantage of these animosities. But this anti-Semitism, both traditional and economic, while certainly real, was not racially based. As Yisrael Gutman puts it, "In Poland, a staunchly Catholic country, even zealous anti-Semites had never dared to promote racist principles" (1982, 59). A possible exception were the Nazi imitators like the ONR. But even among extreme nationalists, there were cases of a change of heart during the war. For example, Jan Mosdorf, jurist and political writer, was one of the founders and leaders of the ONR. His moral integrity and aid to Jewish fellow inmates in Auschwitz was related after the war by several survivors of Auschwitz. Mosdorf was shot there in 1943.[1]

1. Nechama Tec, who as a young girl from Lublin lived for three years on the "Other Side" pretending to be Christian, offers her views on such "changes of heart," including the case of Mosdorf and Rev. Godlewski (1986, 99–112). Another such "Endek" was Henryk Ryszewski, a journalist for anti-Semitic publications before the war, a Christian, who, in his own words, was converted to humanitarianism by the outrageous treatment of the Jews. As a result, he kept thirteen Jews in hiding in his apartment for more than two years. He was awarded the medal of the "Righteous among the Nations" posthumously in 1985. See his candid testimony in Gryberg (2002, 364–69). (His is the only fragment in that collection written by a non-Jew.) See also Friedman (1976, 114–15).

Except for the extreme nationalistic fringe, most of the Poles thought a baptized person was Christian, that is, non-Jewish. Both in the pre-1939 laws, but also in the minds of regular people, Jews were identified, just as Christians were: a Jew belonged to the Mosaic confessional community, and a Christian was a person who belonged to a Roman Catholic, Protestant, or Greek Orthodox confessional community. Other differences like language, customs, economic rivalries, and other protracted conflicts could somehow be negotiated between Jews and Christians. The definitions could be modified through assimilation or conversion, whereas the Nazi racial concept could not. In 1940 simple Jews and simple anti-Semites could not really grasp the Nazi concept.

The complexity of what can collectively be called anti-Semitism can be seen from Czerniaków's entry for July 24, 1941. He writes about meeting a priest: "I returned a visit to Rev. Poplawski who called on me at one time on the subject of assistance to the Christians of Jewish origins. He proceeded to tell me that he sees God's hand in being placed in the ghetto, [but] that after the war he would leave as much an anti-Semite as he was when he arrived there" (1999, 261). But "anti-Semitic" meant many things. Monsignor Seweryn Popławski headed the Nativity of the B.V.M. parish between 1934 and 1944. He refused to leave the ghetto and is known to have helped the persecuted Jews and saved many of them, particularly children. Just before the Polish uprising, the Germans removed him from the church, which they used for storage. He died at seventy-four years of age, during the fighting in August 1944, under the ruins of his church (see Pankiewicz 1997, 77).

People like Rev. Popławski and Rev. Godlewski were profoundly shocked by the Nazis' savage persecutions of the Jews, and of course by the fact that the Nazis considered the baptized Jews to be Jews at all. I fully agree with Rev. Czarnecki's judgment concerning Rev. Godlewski, and probably Rev. Popławski: "Before the War [Rev. Godlewski] was known for his unfriendly [niechętne] attitude toward Jews, but when he saw all the sufferings, he threw himself with all his heart into helping those people" (Czarnecki 1981, 207).

My personal experiences have convinced me that in the face of persecutions and horrors, the attitude toward victim was, in the final analysis, dictated not so much by prewar political convictions as by the mysterious quality of human decency.

———

Establishing the number of Jewish Christians at any moment between the closing of the ghetto and the *Aktion* is difficult. On May 13, 1941, the *Gazeta*

Żydowska (*Jewish Gazette*), a German-controlled Polish-language newspaper for Jews in the GG, wrote that as of January 1, 1941—that is to say, a month and half after the closing of the ghetto—there were 380,740 people living there. Of these, 378,979 were Jews; 1,718 were Catholics, Protestants, or Greek Orthodox; and 43 were of other religious sects (Gutman 1982, 62). It is not clear where the *Jewish Gazette* got this number, but it is quite possible that it came from the census of the Jewish population of Warsaw which the Nazis ordered the *Judenrat* to conduct in the very early stages of the occupation, on October 29, 1939, and which was completed sometime at the end of November of that year. The precise numbers given would certainly indicate that they came from a census, making the *Jewish Gazette* information a year old. The claim that 2,000 Christians lived in the ghetto has often been reiterated, but if it is based on the 1939 census, the number is probably too low. Many Christians who found themselves in the ghetto later were simply not counted by the census takers.

Perhaps more-reliable numbers are those quoted by the present-day parish authorities of the Nativity and All Saints (Revs. Zdzisław Król and Tadeusz Karolak, respectively). The number mentioned is always more than 5,000. Rev. Król, in a conversation with me in March 2001, was definite: "There were 5,200 Christians in the ghetto, most of them Roman Catholic." This number is based on the oral tradition kept in the parishes in lieu of formal documents. The regular registers of all three ghetto parishes were destroyed in the *Aktion,* and the archdiocesan archives were also burned in 1944. These documents were re-created after the war. We have seen that the marginal note in the church register of Saint Augustine (according to the affidavit of Rev. Zygmunt Kowalski) says that there were 5,000 Jewish Christians in the ghetto. A truly reliable reporter of public opinion, Mary Berg, speaks about "several thousand" Christians in the ghetto (1945, 119).

An additional and indirect indication of the number of church-going Christians in the ghetto can be found in Rev. Czarnecki's report on his last Sunday mass in the ghetto: "There was an enormous crowd, such as had never been seen before, in the church [of All Saints]" (1973, 211). According to Rev. Król, the capacity of the church was "3000—full, 4000—crowded." The "enormous crowd" in July 1942, which impressed itself on the memory of Rev. Czarnecki, must in all probability have been more than the "official" number of Christians in the ghetto.

Finally, Philip Friedman, a pioneer Holocaust historian who knew the history of the Warsaw ghetto well, asserts in his study, first published in 1957: "In Warsaw, about more than 6,000 baptized Jews were ordered by the Nazis to move into the ghetto, where they established their own churches. Food parcels were sent to them by the Caritas Cattolica [sic], and several priests moved in to minister to their spiritual needs" (1976, 125).

Part of the reason that the number of Christian Jews given by the *Jewish Gazette* in May 1941 is too low may be that German propaganda wished to diminish the number of persons whose legal Jewish status was certainly shocking, for different reasons, to Jews and to Poles. The *Jewish Gazette* was founded and controlled by the Germans to offer the Jews a false sense of a "normal" self-governing community. It pretended to be strongly "patriotic" in its support of Judaism. Thus on October 7, 1940, it published an appeal to the assimilated and baptized Jews:

> Your way leads not only back, but home. There is a great power in the meaning of this word; there is a deep wisdom in the choice of this way. To return means to experience the rebirth, to discover in oneself the truest germ [*zarodek*], to graft it and to return to the crib, to develop oneself again and to begin from "A" the construction of a new life. Every Jew—even the farthest from Jewishness—carries in himself a grain of Judaism, which constitutes the core of his inner being. . . . The spiritual homeland opens her arms to each lost child. Let us not wait at the threshold! (qtd. in Matywiecki 1994, 466).

This text was printed some five weeks before the sealing off of the ghetto; it is disturbing in its sentimental, deterministic, and racist language. It is racist because it stresses the vaguely biological "rebirth," "germ," "crib," "grain," while passing over in silence the cultural (i.e., historically speaking, religious) origins of the Jewish people.

This Nazi newspaper, written in Polish and destined for a Jewish readership, provides a horrifying example of the Nazis' perverted use of love of folk, nation, and tradition to persuade people to walk into, to run into, the special treatment reserved for Jews. By October 1940 the *Endlösung* was not yet decided, but the special treatment—expulsions, resettlements, ghettoization—certainly was. This appeal also shows how, some seven months later, this newspaper could repeat the old and underestimated number of the "lost children" for "patriotic" reasons.

In trying to estimate the number of Jewish Christians in the ghetto we must also recall that, according to Gutman, "from January to March 1941, about 66,000 Jews from the Warsaw District were transferred to the ghetto . . . by April 1941 there were about 130,000 refugees" (1982, 63).

Some of them were certainly baptized, especially since they came from smaller towns where their origin was better known and the necessity of declaring one's Jewishness was more urgent than in the more anonymous Warsaw. As we shall see, many Jewish Christians were forced into the ghetto in the course of 1941, and there were many baptisms in the ghetto.

I am thus inclined to believe that the number 5,200 is closer to the truth than the 2,000 usually cited, but the destruction of both the parochial and the archdiocesan archives, as well as the discouraging conditions for fact gathering in Poland under the Soviet-sponsored regime, make any definitive estimate probably impossible.

Whatever their exact number, the baptized, recent and old, played, as we shall see, a visible and important role in the life of the Jewish community in the Warsaw ghetto. Although Jewish writers occasionally mentioned converts or seeming converts who were of humble social background, most of the Jewish Christians were recruited from the ranks of assimilated or assimilationist Polish-speaking Jews, who, as we know, were a minority in the population of the Yiddish-speaking Jews. Only the converted or assimilated had any real contact with the Polish intelligentsia, since they belonged to the same class. For this reason, Jewish Christians played an important role in the Warsaw ghetto.

CHAPTER FIVE

Jewish Christians in the Eyes of Jews

It is quite understandable that the popular view of Jewishness and Christianity as indicators of nationality caused the Jewish writers in the ghetto to speak about an "assimilated" (*zasimilowany*), and more often an "assimilationist" (*asymilator*), and a convert (*mekhes*) in the same category. All these terms, the first two Polish, the third Yiddish (used only in Poland), are more or less derogatory. In America, we understand that "convert" can be derogatory, but the term "assimilated" or "assimilationist" is hardly ever used, for most American Jews belong to these categories. Reading the ghetto documents makes it clear that "assimilationist" often implied a person fully at home in the Polish language and culture but also separated from the Jewish people and indifferent to Jewish problems; an "assimilated" Jew implied a person of Polish language and culture not necessarily indifferent to Jewish problems.

The most famous example of the writings from the ghetto by an assimilated Jew is the *Warsaw Diary* of Adam Czerniaków (1999). The *Diary* was written in Polish, with occasional allusions to Polish literary works, and is quite different from other ghetto diaries. Czerniaków wrote a few words virtually every day, and naturally did not present fully finished ideas but rather a series of memoranda for a future history of his chairmanship of the *Judenrat*. These entries are often profoundly moving in their laconism.

Czerniaków was very well informed about the situation in the ghetto, and terse as his observations often are, they are also important in their precise character. His brief notes occasionally mention the converts to Christianity. Although writing in his Polish, he invariably uses the Yiddish term *mekhes* to refer to a convert. His notes echo the main preoccupations of the Christian Jews in the ghetto. He was in constant contact with some of them because some *Judenrat* and *Judenrat*-sponsored offices were filled by converts. As Raul Hilberg et al., editors of the English version of Czerniaków's *Diary*, put it: "Czerniakow was concerned with the professional competence of the applicants for positions. On several occasions, important offices, particularly in the police, were filled with converts to Christianity who had been free in the Polish Republic to pursue careers not open to Jews. Such appointments caused wide-spread resentment in the community and on July 27, 1941, Czerniakow notes that a 4½-hour "fruitless" Council meeting was devoted to this main topic" (Czerniaków 1999, 43).

The idea that the converts were preferred for various offices appears quite often in the ghetto writings. As usual, it is Ringelblum who sums up the problem aptly and succinctly. On April 16, 1941, he notes: "When complaint was made to Czerniakow that, as the head of the Jewish Council, he not only tolerated baptized Jews, but actually placed them in important positions, he replied that he could not approach the problem from the Jewish standpoint, but as one affecting the general government of the ghetto. The ghetto, he said, is not a Jewish state, but an area where baptized Jews are residents, as are Jews—consequently, they must be given equal treatment" (1958, 146–47).

This does not necessarily mean that Czerniaków liked or favored the converts. The first mention of Christians in Czerniaków's diary is probably the shortest of all. On November 19, 1939, he simply jots down: "Baptisms!" (1999, 91). The exclamation mark is eloquent. It may mean that Czerniaków was unpleasantly surprised by the number of baptisms among the Jews who hoped in vain to avoid being classified as Jews. That the Jewish identity of many was not obvious is indicated by the January 6, 1940, entry: "A female convert [*mekheska*] at my home asked me to check if she is listed on the Community rolls, since she does not want to wear the armband" (105–6). On December 6, 1939, he mentions the "List of Christian converts" (97), and on May 13, 1940, "I have received a second list of the baptized" (149). We are not exactly sure what these two lists were, but Marian Fuks, in his introduction to the Polish version of Czerniaków's *Diary*, suggests that: "the Orthodox members of the *Judenrat* attempted to deny the Christian Jews the rights and help given to the Jews. From time to time, they made lists of the *mekheses* in order to exclude them, in some sense, from the "privileges" and services [rendered to other Jews]" (Czerniaków 1983, 27). Czerniaków continues his note of May 13, 1940: "One of the converts told me that his baptism was only temporary; that is, just like a comfortable seat in a streetcar" (1999, 149).

Like many other Jewish ghetto writers, Czerniaków underscores the cynical and materialistic motives for conversion. But as we have seen, by May 1940, four months after the Kott affair, few would really count on a "comfortable seat" among the Christians. Czerniaków duly notes the Kott affair on January 20, 1940, (1999, 109), but without any comments on the larger significance of treating the descendant of a convert as a Jew. The converts are obviously a source of trouble for the *Obmann*. On February 4, 1940, he complains of "throngs of converts" in his office (1999, 114), and on March 4, 1940, he worries that Mrs. Cecylia Oderfeld "has become a convert" (124). His fears were baseless, for this outstanding educator died unbaptized, of typhus, in November 1941 (301).

While Czerniaków may have been disturbed by the sociological phenomenon of conversion, he appreciated the converts' worth and usefulness to the Jewish administration. When, on February 23, 1940, he listened to the various complaints of Dr. Józef Stein, director of the Orthodox hospital on Czyste Street, he did not mention the fact that the doctor was a Christian. He simply overlooked this "defect" in a valuable medical specialist.

On May 29, 1940, Czerniaków explains "in connection with the increasing number of the converts" [in the Polish version: "in the rising wave of the *mekheses*"] that some of them are not converts (1999, 155; Polish, 1983, 116). In other words, he suspected that some persons classified as "converts" were, in fact, not real converts. In support of this opinion, he quotes the entire letter of someone who still lived outside the Jewish quarter and wished to be considered "without religion." This person had nevertheless been classified as a convert. His letter explains that he "did not leave the Jewish Community in 1933 . . . to embrace some better or worse religion, and . . . to list [him] as a baptized Jew . . . is a grievous moral wrong" (1999, 155). Since we know that declarations of "confessionlessness" were extremely rare (Sakowska 1993, 13), it seems that by copying this whole letter, Czerniaków hints at his conviction that conversion was not a religious problem.

On July 29, 1940, he notes: "I have been visited at home by a group of converts who are asking us not to send any more letters to their home addresses requesting contributions to the Community, etc. (they feel ashamed in the presence of their Aryan wives)" (1999, 178). The simpler and truer explanation would be, I believe, that they could not or would not contribute. The "Aryan" wives who accompanied their husbands to the yet unsealed-off ghetto were not ashamed of them. Czerniaków disliked the idea of recent conversions, for on September 1, 1940, he repeated the well-known ghetto joke: "Aryans are either vertical or horizontal. The horizontal ones were carried to their baptism while the vertical ones are walking by themselves" (192). The term "Aryans" is used ironically. Czerniaków knew that by that time the converts, recent or not, were treated as Jews.

While Czerniaków considers the fate of the *mekheses* from the factual, administrative point of view, Emanuel Ringelblum, the unofficial leader of the intellectual opposition to the *Judenrat,* finds in the assimilationists and in the converts a constant source of irritation. Both Czerniaków and Ringelblum express a strongly secular Jewish view of Jewishness, as I have briefly outlined in the introduction. According to this view, a convert is an apostate who has betrayed Jewishness. As secularized persons themselves, neither of them could accept that there was a genuine religious belief or a need of belief behind the conversions. Both simply assumed the more "realistic" explanation that self-interest or a greater or lesser degree of cynicism lay behind the conversions.

For an American reader, Ringelblum's attitude toward the "assimilationists" is perhaps difficult to understand. His is the voice of the secular, assimilated Jew, but certainly not "assimilationist." He was in close touch with Jewish national feelings. He was a progressive "left" Zionist, a member of the Left Po'alei Zion Party. He firmly believed in the separation and coexistence of the Jewish minority and the Polish majority. The cultural autonomy of Jewish life was one of his basic tenets, and this conviction colors all his views about the assimilationists and, of course, Christian Jews.

Like many members of his class Ringelblum was removed from the religious lives of Orthodox Jews. This can be seen in a March 1940 entry: "A Jew could not find a *minyan* in order to say the *Kaddish,* so he boarded the [Jewish] streetcar and recited his prayers [in a required manner]" (Ringelblum 1988a, 117; absent in Ringelblum 1958). The anecdote is a mildly humorous comment on a novelty—the streetcars reserved exclusively for Jews— but it demonstrates a lack of serious consideration for the religious obligation of the *minyan,* or for the religious significance of the prayers in praise of the creator of life to be recited on the anniversary of a death. As a secularized person, and a convinced Marxist, Ringelblum does not talk about any search for a religious sense of life.

But he certainly took his Jewishness seriously. Perhaps the best way to understand Ringelblum's basic views about Jewishness is to read what he says when he is not speaking about the Polish Jews but about the fate of those who live in the Soviet Union. This entry from May 1942 was written when the reputation of the Soviet Union was at its zenith: "Without territorial concentration we are condemned—it appears—to complete assimilation, unless the revolution creates new possibilities for national development. There is not much hope, because the news that we receive from over there [the USSR] confirms a total assimilation: the schools in Kiev, Mińsk and other cities [with large Jewish populations] have been closed. The only center of Jewish culture is the theater. There is no Jewish learning there" (1988a, 388; absent in Ringelblum 1958).

Ringelblum was certainly conscious of the *mekhes* phenomenon, and more than anyone else—with the possible exception of Marian Małowist (see below)—he associated the assimilationists with the converts, for assimilationists are converts to another culture. Although I am sure that this highly educated and intelligent man understood the philosophical distinctions between these categories, in his hastily jotted notes written in the chaotic and terrifying atmosphere of the ghetto, he simply had no time for them. (Note in this connection that some entries bear two or more dates, which means that he started to jot down an entry one day only to finish it on the next.)

Ringelblum, like Czerniaków, intended, I am sure, his notes to serve as materials for a future study of the ghetto. He was very interested in popular opinion and at the beginning of the German occupation, in his entry of February 1, 2, 1940, he notes what Jewish children, perhaps sensing the horrors to come, were predicting: "According to [my son] Uri, the children tell one another: 'The old people will be shot, the middle-aged will be sent to the camps, and the children will be baptized and passed out among Christian families'" (1958, 15).

His entry for March 9, 12, 15, 16, 1940, reports the growing numbers of baptisms and gives his reason for them: "Since last November more than 200 Jews have accepted baptism in Warsaw, among them Marek Orensztajn and Watong.[1] You can also find—besides doctors and representatives of other free professions—a small shopkeeper from Mokotów and others. The reason: converts receive visas for permanent residence in Italy, and in Warsaw they receive white bread (54 [visas] in January)" (1988a, 101–2; absent in Ringelblum 1958). There was, indeed, some emigration to the still neutral Italy, and even to Palestine at the beginning of 1940, but one did not have to be a "Christian" to receive a visa. The Germans simply demanded a great deal of

1. Marek Orensztajn (or Arensztajn) was a well-known actor and director who directed a Polish-language theater in the ghetto under his theater name, Andrzej Marek. Watong was also a theater person. A year and a half later (November 1941), Ringelblum mentions the theater, but having forgotten Marek's name: ". . . the director of the Polish-language theater at 52 Nowolipki Street. He supposed to be a baptized Jew, name unknown. The star of the theater is the popular Michael Znicz, also a convert" (1958, 231).

hard currency for this privilege. As for white bread, it was a rarity as much in
the "Aryan" as in the Jewish section, since the production of wheat bread
was officially forbidden in Poland, but there is no reason to believe that Ringelblum knew about this. While reading the reactions of the ghetto dwellers,
especially after its closing (November 29–December 2, 1940), we must remember that there was a tendency to consider life outside the ghetto as a paradise. We shall see this in the memoirs of a Protestant ghetto dweller, Antoni
Marianowicz (1995). There is a common human tendency to make absolute
the relative differences in misery. I myself remember my stay in Stalag XB in
northwestern Germany. In April of 1945 the SS dumped into this grim military
camp hundreds of Neuengamme concentration camp inmates. The reaction
of these mistreated and starving men was that our stalag was "heaven," because, they said, we ate something twice a day *every day.*

In the entry for December 12, 13, 14, 1940, Ringelblum observes what he
considers a growing phenomenon:

> The problem of the baptized Jews is becoming more real in the
> ghetto. Many very gifted persons, who used to hold leading positions
> in Poland have joined the medical milieu [of the ghetto]. Now, they
> pretend to hold leading positions in Jewish life. The sentimental doc-
> tor [Izrael] M[ilejkowski], the Head of the Department of Health
> [in the *Judenrat*] quipped: "*Mekheses* have an inferiority complex to-
> ward the Christians and manifest a megalomania toward the Jews."
> We can give them bread, we can share every last bit of it, but they will
> not decide about the life of the Jewish population. (1988a, 214–15;
> absent in Ringelblum 1958)

But Ringelblum does not seem to be unduly disturbed by this drive for power
by the converts because on the same page he notes: "The baptized Jews, hap-
pily, do not attempt to become leaders in the life of the Jewish population."

Perhaps the greatest fault of the converts is that they help in the assimilationist process, as Ringelblum observes in the entry dated April 6, 1941:
"Some people have pointed out that, rather than the baptized Jews assimilating to the Jews, a contrary process is taking place, particularly on Sienna
Street [on the southern border of the ghetto, close to the All Saints Church]
where the converts comprise a significant part of all residents. They are influ-
encing the Jews to become more assimilationist. On the other hand young
converts made a ceremony of putting on Jewish Star arm bands. There was
speech making for the occasion" (1958, 147). The last two sentences, though

they are a non sequitur, are important, for the religious and political situation was surely more complex than these simple materialistic explanations implied. We must be aware that here, as in many places in his journal, Ringelblum does not analyze, he simply records the information received and offers his immediate reactions.

Before the war, Ringelblum belonged to the group of historians associated with the Commission for Jewish History at YIVO in Vilna. The commission was one of the centers of Marxist thought in Poland (Leociak 1997, 40). To the very end of the ghetto, Ringelblum ascribed various simple, materialistic (Marxist, so to speak) motives to every manifestation of the complex phenomenon of Christianization and stressed the privileged situation of the converts. In the entry for March 18, 1941, he observes: "There are a hundred baptized Jews serving in the police force in prominent positions. They are also thrusting their way into chairs of responsibility in the House Committees, particularly in the Fifth District. Their neighbors are debating whether or not to permit them to hold important positions. In the church on Grzybow Place [Grzybowski Square] one of the baptized Jewish policemen shouted: 'Down with the Jews!' It was impossible to establish who he was. But that's characteristic of their arrogance" (1958, 138–39). In a similar vein, he complains in his entry of mid-September 1941:

> The converts are to have a separate school of their own. There was a big controversy over this school. [Abraham] Gepner [member of the *Judenrat,* director of the Supply Office] maintained that, for political considerations, the baptized Jews ought to attend common schools, but they should have special religious instruction. The neophytes do not want these schools, they want schools of their own, and they will get them, because they get whatever they ask. They get as many [soup] lunches as they wish, even the rich get them. Even if they have recently done us a "favor": their Caritas accepts the Jews as consumers, [the converts] receive more produce than everyone else, lately [they got] 4 or 6 kilos of sugar. They occupy the most important positions in the Jewish Community [*Judenrat*], in the police, etc. They support one another. They push their way into everything and they are quite successful in it. Some of the rabbis and the people from the nationalist circles tried to put up a fight. They called meetings, but so far there are no results. I have heard that when a neophyte was asked why he had converted in wartime, he answered "to get a bigger bread ration." Even now there are rumors that there

are cases of baptism in the ghetto. I could not ascertain how true these rumors are. (1988a, 317–18; slightly different in Ringelblum 1958, 213–14)

Let me observe that in September 1941, four or six kilograms of sugar per person was a quantity that could have existed only in wishful and hungry imagination, either in the ghetto or on the "Other Side." Caritas did distribute help to the converts and to others, but it was not on such a large scale as Ringelblum and other ghetto writers imply. Rev. Czarnecki presents the quite modest dimension of this aid:

> The director of Caritas offered the parish of All Saints help in cash and in kind. Unfortunately the guards controlling the ghetto gate on Żelazna and Grzybowska frequently confiscated the food brought by bicycle "rickshaw." In spite of these difficulties and the irregular supply of food, our kitchen gave out up to one hundred portions [of soup] every day to all who came, without considering their faith. The action ended when the Germans forbade anyone to help the Jews on pain of death. This was at the beginning of November 1941. But even then, the parish still helped those in extreme need. (1981, 207–8)

In October 1941, Ringelblum repeats the disturbing rumors of baptisms in the ghetto and offers his usual explanation of this phenomenon: "A great many cases of change of faith. On the day of Hoshana Raba more than fifty Jews were converted (numbers furnished by the *Judenrat*). The reason: Caritas looks after the neophytes. Hope that the converts will be able to leave the ghetto. There was even some talk of a converts' ghetto in Zoliborz. One hears a joke: 'Do you want a job in the Jewish Community Council? Get baptized.' Apart from everything else, this is a psychopathological phenomenon" (1988a, 327; the last sentence missing in Ringelblum 1958, 226).

In the same October 1941 entry, while talking about the shrinking area of the ghetto, Ringelblum stresses the economically privileged status of the converts:

> Neophyte Avenue, on Sienna Street, with its row of fine modern houses with central heating, was excluded from the ghetto. In general, Sienna was the street where the Jewish aristocracy lived. A broad street, with good air, little poverty, few beggars, kept clean—literally,

an island in the ghetto. In the evening you could see well-dressed women, wearing lipstick and rouge, strolling calmly down the street with their dogs, as though there was no war. There was none of the confinement, hullabaloo, or nervousness of the ghetto here. An isle of repose. A survival of the expansiveness of prewar life in the middle of the ghetto. (1958, 222)

Some of Ringelblum's views and opinions are shared by Stefan Ernest. Ernest is perhaps more analytic and more detached in discussing the inhabitants of Sienna Street. I find it significant that he does not even use the term "convert" or, for that matter, "Christian" or "baptized." He completely identifies assimilated Jews with baptized ones:

I must add here that Sienna Street . . . constituted, socially speaking, a separate district. Here lived those persons who had nothing or very little to do with Jewry, except for the formal belonging to the Mosaic faith—but even here there were exceptions. These persons encountered many difficulties in adapting psychologically. They were strangers to the rest of the ghetto, and the ghetto was foreign to them. These persons suffered the most. Some of them, as a sign of protest, never left their dwellings. This happened more in the Sienna Street district than elsewhere. These people were tied to Polish society by family or social relations, friendship, and often by marriage. They often crossed to the Aryan side; as to their own people, they escaped as they say, from the Jews. For they were Jews only from the point of view of the German legislation. During their stay in the ghetto the majority of them received assistance from parishes and attended religious services in the two ghetto churches: the Carmelite church [the Church of the Nativity of the B.V.M.] and All Saints. (2003, 127–28)

Ernest seems to be more detached and less disapproving of the privileged inhabitants of Sienna Street than Ringelblum. It is probably not a question of personal opinion; his different tone in describing Sienna Street probably results from the date of his writing. Ringelblum was writing in October of 1941, when no one could really predict the fate of the ghetto, but Ernest is attempting to describe the ghetto after its final destruction. The differences between the converts and the Jews, the privileged and the helpless, became less important after the *Aktion* and the final overcoming of Jewish resistance. This is clearly perceivable in his conclusion to this section: "Many of them shared the fate of those who went to Treblinka, the others gradually penetrated to the 'Other Side.' Together with those who never went to the ghetto, they, the majority of them, will not wish to be counted as Jews. In the meanwhile they constitute a group apart, although, with the passing of time, some of them accepted positions in the *Judenrat* and in the Jewish Order Service" (2003, 128). But even when, in October 1941, the Germans cut the southern side of the Sienna Street district off from the ghetto, and the converts lost half of their "isle of repose" and many of them had to seek new lodgings in the ghetto, they still remained privileged in Ringelblum's eyes. He and others saw the converts as simply a strange, materialistically minded separate group who tended to behave as any disliked and self-encapsulated group would behave.

Piotr Matywiecki, an important commentator on the Shoah in Poland, and himself the son of converts, conceived in the ghetto but born on the "Other Side," suggests more: "It would be easy to say that for the Jewish community on the whole the neophytes were what the Jews [were] in the non-Jewish world. There is much to be said for it. Both groups were a *sign* of otherness. They stressed, willingly or not, their separateness perpetuating it through their double complex of inferiority and superiority. . . . Both were accused of sticking together and supporting their own" (1994, 467). Ultimately, Matywiecki sees both "anti-*mehesism*" and anti-Semitism as manifestations of a general human tendency: "The natural irreflectiveness [*bezreflek-syjność*] of life tempts us to separate ours from others. The alive from the condemned?" (468).

Reading Ringelblum, one sometimes gets the impression that when the ghetto was sealed off, the Jewish Christians were envied for another reason, namely, for their greater facility of hiding in the "Aryan" world. This is also implied in Ernest's conclusion. Both were right in this respect. As early as November 15, 1940, Ringelblum notes: "A baptized Jew, Grajerzon (?) lives in an apartment house on 32 Elektoralna Street. His daughters, ardent anti-Semites, must wear Jewish armbands. [But] other baptized Jews moved to small towns, changed their names and addresses, etc." (1988a, 196; absent in Ringelblum 1958). The greatest value of Ringelblum's notes, jotted down hastily and without time for analysis, is precisely that they refer to such incidents as this. Rumors reported by Ringelblum were as abundant in the Warsaw ghetto as in any other coerced society (*Zwangsgesellschaft*).

Right after the closing of the ghetto, he notes a wishful rumor: "They say that in the church on Grzybowski Square, there was a service for the baptized Jews. It was expected that the priest [Marceli Godlewski] would announce in his sermon that the baptized Jews could leave the ghetto, but the announcement did not take place" (1988a, 209; absent in Ringelblum 1958). A year later in the entry for December 24, 25, 1941, he repeats the rumor, which is clearly marked with "they say": "They say that today, on Christmas Day, 24–25 of December, during the religious service, the priest is alleged to have said that the neophytes should disown the Jews [żeby wyparli się]. The Jewish police kept order" (1988a, 341; absent in Ringelblum 1958). This rumor was indeed just that. From what we know about the two parishes in the ghetto, it seems to me impossible that one of the priests could have said this. What could have been said was something like: "The neophytes should firmly safeguard their Christian faith."

Sometimes Ringelblum repeats news from the "Other Side" which is pertinent to our subject. For example, on December 31, 1940, he reports: "Heard there have been demonstrations the last few days in Polish cities, the demonstrators' slogan 'No Jews in Warsaw.' But heard at the same time sermons have been preached in all the churches urging Christians to forget their misunderstanding with the Jews. On the contrary, the Jews are to be pitied because they are immured behind the walls. Christians were not to allow themselves to be agitated by the enemy, who was trying to sow hatred among peoples" (1958, 117).

Only two and half months later, on February, 27, 28, 1941, Ringelblum notes: "Several days ago (February 23–28) there was a welcoming ceremony of more than 20 families, who were on the list of Ronikier. Among them were Benedykt Hertz, professor [Ludwik] Hirszfeld, Dr. [Aleksander] Wertheim and others. In the Jewish Council, they prepared the armbands for them" (1988a, 236; absent in Ringelblum 1958). And on the next page, he repeats: "Among converts who moved in [to the ghetto] are Professor Hirszfeld, well known in Europe as an authority in the field of bacteriology, and Natanson. Czerniaków showed Natanson the portrait of his grandfather [Ludwik Natanson, the president of the Jewish community, 1871–96]. The grandson acknowledged that his grandfather had acted better than he [by not converting]" (1988a, 237; slightly different in Ringelblum 1958, 129). The idea that the *mekheses* apologized or gave cynical reasons for their conversion was firmly anchored in Ringelblum's mind. This was for him the only possible and immediate explanation for this otherwise "psychopathological phenomenon."

People on the "Other Side," that is, in the society that attracts the conversions, are also presented as "greedy" for converts. In one of the later entries, on December 5, 1942, three months after the end of the *Aktion,* he briefly observes: "Children: Christian missions took advantage of the situation to baptize Jewish children. Many of the cloisters accepted Jewish children especially girls, and baptized them" (1988a, 425; absent in Ringelblum 1958). Ringelblum had his facts right, if not their motivation. Ewa Kurek, a serious scholar, published a dissertation the subject which has recently been translated into English (1997).[2] Girls were preferred by the rescuers, because the boys bore the identifying mark of circumcision. Three months after the *Aktion,* there was a painful debate in the residual ghetto concerning the fate of the children sent to Catholic orphanages. The whole long entry of December 14, 1942, is devoted to that subject. Since it touches directly on Jewish attitudes toward the Catholic Church in general and the converts in particular, it must be quoted here:

> Priests wish to rescue Jewish Children.
> In certain circles a plan is now under discussion to rescue a certain number (several hundred) of Jewish children by placing them in monasteries in various parts of the country. Three factors motivated the men of the cloth to propose this: first, soul snatching. The Catholic religious leaders have always exploited such difficult moments in Jewish life as pogroms, deportations, etc., to convert adults and children. This is perhaps the most important factor motivating the proposal, although the clergy assure us that they will not attempt to convert the Jewish children entrusted to the care of their institutions.
> There is a second, *economic* factor. Every Jewish child will have to pay 600 zlotys a month, and for a year in advance too. This is a very good stroke of business for the monastic orders; since they have their fields and gardens, their food costs are low. For the Jewish children who are unable to meet this fee, costs are to be covered by the children of the rich who will be taxed double.
> The third factor is that of prestige. Until now, the Polish Christian spiritual leaders have done very little to save Jews from massacre

2. In 2001 Kurek published an enlarged edition in Polish of her 1992 book under a different title. The 1992 text is followed by an appendix (111–240) containing testimonies of both rescued and rescuers. For additional testimonies of those who survived in one of the cloisters, see Gawryś (1998). See also the balanced appraisal of the role of the church in the rescuing effort, presented from the Jewish point of view, by Tec (1986, 136–49).

and "resettlement," to use Their [German] euphemism. In view of the worldwide protest against the mass murder of Polish Jews, rescuing several hundred Jewish children may be offered as evidence that the Polish clergy did not sit with hands folded in these difficult times, that they did everything they could to help the Jews, particularly their children.

I was present at a discussion by several Jewish intellectuals. One of them categorically opposed the operation. He argued that though it was agreed that [only] children between ten and fourteen years of age were to be put in the convents (as desired by the Jewish negotiators), the children—*though supposedly old enough to resist indoctrination*—[words in italics not in Ringelblum 1988a] would fall under the priests' influence and would be converted sooner or later. The priests' promise not to convert the children would be of no avail; time and education would take their toll. He maintained that we must follow the example of our fathers and accept martyrdom in His name ["and die for the faith," Ringelblum 1988a]. We have no right to give our blessing to the conversion of our children. Jewish society has no right to engage in such an enterprise. Let it be left to every individual to decide and to act on an individual basis.

When, he concluded, 300,000 Jews have been exterminated in Warsaw, what avail is it to rescue several hundred children? Let them perish or survive together with the rest of their people.

However, others argued: We must look after the future. In time of massacre such as this, with all European Jewry being slaughtered, the soul of each and every Jew is precious, and we must take pains to try and preserve it. After the war, the clergy will have no influence. Who knows whether they will even exist.[3] This being so, there is no need to fear lest the children fall under the influence of the monastic orders. When one studies the pages of Jewish history closely, one discovers that martyrdom in His name[4] was not the principle of our history. On the contrary, marranism was pseudo-Christianity. Jews have always adapted themselves to the hardest conditions, have always known how to survive the hardest times. Sending a handful of

3. This statement foresees a thoroughly Sovietized Poland after the war.
4. The Polish text here and in the second paragraph above, gives "death for the faith." Both "to die in His name" and "to die for the faith" express the concept of the *Kiddush ha-shem* (lit. "Sanctification of the Name").

Jewish children into the monasteries will enable us to rescue those who will be creators of a new generation of Jews. We have no right to take away the coming generation's right to live.

Those who took this position argued that [words in italics not in Ringelblum 1988a] one must strongly underline the difference between conversion and pseudo-Christianity. The priests themselves state that the children will not be converted, but will have to conduct themselves outwardly like Christians. True, there is some danger that if this persists for a long time some of the children will fall under the influence of the clergy—but there is a second, worse danger. If we do not carry out this child-rescue operation with the aid of the clergy, in a short time none will remain, the handful whom we are now in position to rescue will perish as well. Numbers, some of the intellectuals said, are the most important consideration at this time. At any cost, we must rescue the largest possible number of Jews: so we must agree to the proposal to place some of our children in convents.

Still others argued that the thing had to be done, but not with the sanction of the representative of Jewish society. Individuals were rescuing themselves in various ways—let the convent be matter of individual choice. (1958, 336–38; Ringelblum 1988a, 434–36)

This long entry is a real essay, rather than a hastily jotted note. It was written by Ringelblum when he was confronting the total annihilation of the ghetto. It is a reasoned presentation of his views on Christianization. There is no doubt in my mind that he agreed with the opinions expressed in the last paragraph.

Ringelblum repeated the substance of this discussion in his Polish book written in hiding on the "Other Side." We learn there that the discussants were social workers. Ringelblum's reiteration ends with a sad conclusion: "The project was not carried out, because of a variety of difficulties, but mainly because the Polish clergy was not much interested in the question of saving Jewish children" (1992, 150–51). I know that his conclusion is not accurate: the "variety of difficulties," which included the fear of death, were more important, I believe, than the lack of interest on the part of those reputed "soul snatchers."

The debate among the social workers in the ghetto requires some comment. First, the nuns who ran the orphanages did so chiefly of their own accord and sometimes with only the tacit approval of the Catholic hierarchy. To safeguard the life of the rescued and the rescuers, the children had to be rescued under the rules for all underground activities. For security reasons, the hierarchy wished to know as little as possible. Indeed, the *Aktion* in Warsaw caused a rallying of the helpers. It was then that the Żegota organization came to life.

Second, most of the convents running the orphanages were very poor, and accepting some paying orphans was important to them. They and their orphans lived on the charity of an impoverished Polish population.

Third, whatever the motivation of the clergy, either lucre or prestige, there was a death sentence for giving any form of help to Jews. The sentence was formally promulgated by the edict of the general governor of the GG, Hans Frank, on October 15, 1941. It stipulated death both for Jews leaving the ghetto and for all persons helping them in any way whatsoever. In fact, helpers were regularly killed before October 15, 1941, but the death sentence was applied with particular ruthlessness from the summer of 1942 on, that is, at the same time that the numbers of escapes from the ghetto sharply increased. Let me emphasize this point for the last time: in Poland (and in the occupied territory of the Soviet Union) any assistance rendered to a Jew was punishable by death, a sentence extended to members of the household, often including children and servants. Thus, in Poland any help offered to Jews had to be based on something more serious than financial gain or prestige. Any decision to help had to be weighed against the very real threat of death for the helpers and their families.

Had Anne Frank not been Dutch but Polish, and had her betrayer not been a Dutch collaborator but a Polish *szmalcownik,* the "Aryans"—two women and two men responsible for the hiding place in the "Annex"—would have died with her and with the seven other Jews. In the Dutch case, the two women were not arrested at all. One of them immediately went to the un-sealed "Annex" and rescued Anne Frank's manuscript. The two men were arrested by the Dutch, but one was released immediately on account of his bad health. The second escaped from the work camp before it was evacuated to Germany in January 1945.

Fourth, there is a fact which is well known now but which Ringelblum and his fellow ghetto dwellers simply did not know, or if they did hear it they could not believe it: that in December 1942 there were no worldwide protests about the annihilation of the Jews. The Polish government-in-exile was well informed. By January 1942 it had already published, in London, a book called *The German Order in Poland,* part 3 of which presented a detailed report on the persecution of the Polish Jews.

Jan Karski, one of the Righteous among the Nations, was a Polish courier for the AK. He came to England in November 1942 and later to the United States with detailed information about the annihilation of the Polish Jews.

Before his mission abroad, disguised as a French worker going to France on a furlough, he spent some time in the Bełżec annihilation camp posing as a Latvian guard. Later, he was smuggled into the Warsaw ghetto and received messages from the underground Jewish leaders. In Britain and in the United States, he met with several important political personalities. On December 10, 1942, the Polish government-in-exile sent a long and detailed document entitled *The Mass Extermination of Jews in Occupied Poland* to all the Allied governments. Neither the published documents nor Karski's revelations attracted much attention or, perhaps, much credence.[5] The Soviet authorities never specifically mentioned the Shoah. They spoke only about Nazi persecutions of the civilian population.

Fifth, Ringelblum repeats that the priests did promise not to baptize the children. Subsequent events proved that in large part they kept their promises. The baptized (or supposedly baptized) children were told who they were after the war, and their Christianization was explained to them. Ewa Kurek, knowledgeable historian, emphasizes this point over and over in her studies (1997; 2001). After spending years studying the fate of Jewish children rescued by religious, she does not know of any case in which the Jewish origin of the child was not revealed after the war. Most of the children left Poland in the 1940s and the 1950s, either to join relatives abroad or to go to orphanages in Israel or elsewhere. Those who stayed in their adopted environment were usually older orphans who made the decision to stay on their own. In this last group there are some persons who have not been willing to reveal their origin.[6]

---

5. For the reception of the news from Poland about the ongoing Shoah, as well as for Karski's mission, see Laqueur (1981, 101–22, 219–38); see also Wood and Jankowski (1994).

6. At the begining of her study of Christian rescuers, Nechama Tec presents succinctly the psychological dilemma of some of the rescued. She describes one of her telephone conversations:

> I introduced myself, explained the study, and told him that since he was a Holocaust survivor who had passed as a Christian, I would like to interview him. I was still explaining when he interrupted me: "My past is my own business, it is too private to be used by anyone . . ." I tried to point to the need, the importance, but there was barely time, for his angry, rough voice cut me short: "You heard me, I will not be a part of your study. My innermost feelings are not for exhibition, not for show . . ." His tone more than his words was a warning. Shaken and embarrassed, I hung up. And yet, I could identify with him. (1986, vi)

It is important to realize that Tec conducted her interviews of the rescued and rescuers in Poland between 1978 and 1980, during the stormy months leading to the formation of Solidarity, which could further explain an increased reluctance on the part of some survivors to talk about their past.

Sixth, as I mentioned in the introduction, Marranism as a life-saving solution was not really applicable in 1942 Warsaw. In Warsaw, a change of religion,
whether pretended or real, did not guarantee protection from being considered Jew by the Nazis. It did help in hiding among the majority. It afforded a
kind of camouflage, but only to those who were thoroughly assimilated. There
are, alas, no real historical antecedents that Ringelblum could have cited here.

I believe that Ringelblum was not alone in the ghetto in having such
feelings toward the Christian Jews. In the horrible physical and psychological
conditions of any coerced living situation there is an exaggerated envy of privileged individuals or groups. Much of this antagonism stemmed from envy of
the real or supposed privileges that the *mekheses* received, the help from Caritas, and the "favorable" treatment they enjoyed from the *Judenrat* authorities.
It also came from the sentiment that conversions were largely mercenary in
nature. And as might be expected, the reaction of simple, especially religious,
people was more violent. In the memoir of Stanisław Gajewski, preserved in
the archives of Yad Vashem, there is a description of an incident during the
Sunday mass in the All Saints Church: ". . . a big crowd of Hasidim gathered
outside. They were waiting . . . for those Jewish-Catholics to leave the church
in order to beat them up. They carried sticks. The [Jewish] Order Service was
called. The policemen got into action with the cry: 'They are beating our
Jews' and began to use their sticks on the Hasidim . . . who wanted to lynch
the others [*mekheses*]" (qtd. in Engelking and Leociak 2001, 622).

Occasionally, for instance in his entry for December 15, 17, 20, 1940,
Ringelblum shows a sympathy, at least toward the "old" converts: "It is said
that the priest who came to the ghetto Sunday to preach to the converts was
allowed [Ringelblum 1958: "was not allowed"] to pass through the gate. Some
were converted as long as forty to sixty years ago, and now they must suffer
the Jewish exile in the ghetto. Some of them have had to separate from their
Aryan wives, who have remained behind on the 'Other Side'" (1988a, 217–18;
Ringelblum 1958, 109). In his *Relations*, written while in hiding on the "Aryan"
side, at the end of the section dealing with the attitudes of the Polish clergy
toward the Jews, Ringelblum outlines the general situation of the converts
in the ghetto, and then mentions the genuinely religious ones. But even here,
his attitude toward a manifestation of piety contains a touch of irony or
sarcasm:

> In the ghetto, the Catholic clergy took care of them [converts]. They
> were given the use of the blocks of flats belonging to the parishes
> on Leszno Street and in the Grzybow district. In the Church of All

Saints in the Grzybow [Grzybowki Square] and in the Church of [the Nativity] of the Holy Virgin Mary on Leszno Street, Catholic services were held with the participation of convert church attendants and a converts' choir. Real believers could be seen in these churches. Women zealots lay prostrate on the floor [Polish, p. 149: *leżały plackiem na ziemi*, "were down on the ground, flat like pancakes"], praying fervently. (1992, 210)

In general I believe it can be said that Ringelblum, although he shared an agelong negative attitude toward the apostate that I mentioned in the introduction, was a well-trained historian, careful to distinguish between what he knew and what he heard even in his hastily written notes. He viewed the Christian Jews in the ghetto negatively, but with fairness.

There is no doubt that for many of the ghetto memorialists the Christians among them were a curiosity more than anything else. An example of such an attitude can be found in Chaim Hasenfus's diary, fragments of which were recently published by Michał Grynberg (2002, 31–38). Hasenfus was an assimilated university graduate in philology, and a prewar bank employee. He left a few dated entries of his ghetto memoir, which ended on September 30, 1941. Nothing is known about the fate of the author after that date. Under May 11, 1941, he notes:

I had a conversation—typical of the times—with three ladies who had recently been released from prison. They had been sent there for several months for not wearing armbands or for living outside the ghetto. All three were wealthy and well educated; all were Catholics—one was even born into that faith. The Germans turned them back into Jews. One of the ladies explained that most of the women in prison were Jews who had been christened, the wives of Polish officers. Twenty-five people are kept in one cell. The daughter of the second lady is still in prison and the husband of the third was sent to a prison in Siedlce. All three talked about passing secret messages, and the whole experience of prison made such an impression on the youngest that she's collecting literary accounts of prison experiences. They claimed that in general they were better off there than in the ghetto. (Grynberg 2002, 36)

Mary Berg, whom I have already mentioned, was far less detached in her memoir (1945). Let us recall that she was the daughter of an American mother and a Polish Jewish father. She went to the ghetto in its early period and lived there until the *Aktion,* when she was imprisoned with other foreign nationals in Pawiak prison. She left Poland in January 1943 to be exchanged for Germans held by the Americans, and arrived in the United States in March 1944. During her stay in Warsaw and after, she wrote the notes for her diary in Polish, often in a cryptic form. Once in America she rewrote them. They were translated and published immediately. This intelligent teenager mentions Christian Jews several times, and she seems to have echoed the opinions and rumors current among assimilated Jews.

On December 11, 1941, two months after her seventeenth birthday, she noticed the presence of Jewish Christians in the ghetto:

> Today I learned many interesting details about a quite sepa-
> rate little world of the ghetto. These are the converts, who are per-
> haps the most tragic figures among us. I had seen them on several
> occasions, but until now I had no close contact with them. Recently
> I came to know them through Julia Tarnowska, a student in one of
> the lower grades in our school.
>
> Julia is the daughter of the writer Marceli Tarnowski. She is an
> eccentric and likes to attract attention. The very first day she came to
> school I had a clash with her on the subject of her Jewish origin.
>
> Julia, like her parents, is a convert. She learned of her Jewish
> origin only when her family received the order to move out of their
> apartment on the "Aryan" side and take up quarters in the ghetto.
> This incident shook her deeply, and she has not yet resigned herself
> to her fate. She is constantly indignant and angry, and I have a feel-
> ing that she is more resentful against the Jews than the Nazis. She
> considers her lot the result of a fatal mistake, for which I and others
> like me are responsible.
>
> Around her neck she wears a large silver cross, and she tries to
> persuade everyone that she is a faithful Christian who has nothing
> in common with Judaism. (1945, 118)

After reminding Julia that she was wrong to feel ashamed of being Jewish, for she observed that "Christ, too, was a Jew but was never ashamed of his origin" (118), Mary began to ponder the fate of other converts: "Because of the incident with Julia . . . I became interested in the Jewish Christians in the ghetto. Their number now reached several thousands, and the Nazis have brought them together from several countries. The majority are converts of the 'Hitler period,' that is to say, those who went over to Christianity during the very recent years, hoping to escape the fate of the persecuted Jews" (119). Mary Berg assumes that the children of converts are being brought up to be anti-Semites, again expressing a view largely held by most of her elders: "There are also converts who left the Jewish faith decades ago, and whose children were brought up as pious Christians. These children are accustomed to go to church every Sunday, and their souls were even poisoned with anti-Semitism taught them by their own parents, who thus tried to eradicate every trace of their Jewish origin" (119). But she does feel sorry for them: "These Christian-born children of Jewish parents are now living through a double tragedy as compared with Jewish children. They feel entirely lost, and there have been cases of suicide among them, while there have been no such cases among Jewish youth" (119).

The subject of suicides among the population of the ghetto would certainly require a book-length monograph. There were numerous cases of suicide in the ghetto, but Mary's statement concerning a higher rate of suicide among Christian Jewish children has not been expressed, as far as I could ascertain, by any other witness. She ends her discussion of the converts in the ghetto, on the same page, with another strange and unconfirmed bit of information that some Christians of more distant Jewish origin went voluntarily not only to the ghetto but also back to Judaism, "because of the Nazis' ferocious persecution of the Jews." She also talks about the various privileges supposedly enjoyed by the converts.

A different sort of diarist is Stanisław Adler. In his Polish-language memoirs from the ghetto he does not repeat hearsay. He shares the lucidity of Ringelblum, but his account of those horrible times is unemotional and somehow detached. Adler was a thoroughly assimilated Jew and a lawyer by profession. He lived among assimilated and Christianized Jews. He was an officer in the Jewish Order Service, and as such had access to all sorts of information. His book is particularly important for the history of the *Judenrat* and the Jewish police. Not willing to participate in rounding up the victims to the *Umschlagplatz*, he resigned from the police at the beginning of the *Aktion*. Later he headed the Office of Housing. When he found himself in the residual ghetto, his office became obsolete. By then the *Judenrat* had lost whatever executive power it had, and the occupier governed the ghetto almost exclusively through the Jewish Order Service. Assured by the new head of the *Judenrat*, Marek Lichtenbaum, that his usefulness was over, he escaped with his friend Dr. Ludmiła Zełdowicz to the "Aryan" side, where they were sheltered by several, mostly leftist, friends. They survived despite several near scrapes with death.

Like Ludwik Hirszfeld, Adler wrote his memoirs after his escape from the ghetto in February 1943 and before the liberation in late 1944. Its original and unwieldy title was *A Chronicle of the Events Which Led to the Extermination of the Jewish Population in Warsaw, Poland*. After the war, Dr. Zełdowicz emigrated to the West, taking the complete manuscript with her, and was influential in its publication in English. Adler became more and more despondent—not an unusual fate for a survivor—and shot himself on July 11, 1946.

Adler's book gives a succinct but exact account of the "Ronikiers":

> I speak of that group of baptized Jews who had remained outside the ghetto when the Jewish Quarter had been formed, thanks to the presentations of their primary guardian, its chairman, the *padre* Adam Ronikier. To this group belonged prominent intellectuals, scholars, lawyers, physicians, and top-ranking officials. The Germans, with their usual perfidy, consented to these people remaining outside the ghetto, provided that they were subject to strict regulations; otherwise, they formed an element which could hide from the Gestapo with relative ease through contacts with friends and eventually through support by the Aryan population. The Germans were successful with their trap; a considerable number of individuals secured "Ronikier" certificates and were subsequently captured by the Gestapo and thrown into the ghetto. (1982, 169).

The word *padre* is used ironically by Adler. Adam Ronikier was not a priest, but a conservative Catholic.

Adler discusses the "Ronikiers" in terms of the internal struggle of the *Judenrat* to name an appropriate candidate for the disciplinary magistrate. Finally Mieczysław Adam Ettinger was named:

> He was considered to be the most outstanding expert in Poland. From a legal point of view, no objection could be raised. . . . Nevertheless, the real storm exploded in the Jewish Council over his candidature. His adversaries had basic objections. They maintained that a baptized Jew should not—as in Ettinger's case—in this most tragic period for the Jewish people under German occupation, be appointed to such an important post. The First Magistrate, they claimed, should

be the exponent of the "highest ethics" that could be held by an employee of the Jewish self-governing institution and not by an individual who had committed the act of changing religion for reasons which, under the circumstances, were considered to be opportunistic. The storm caused by Ettinger's nomination did not subside for a long time. (1982, 170)

Czerniaków also mentions the controversy caused by this nomination, which he favored, in his entries for July 2 and 27, 1941 (1999, 254, 262–63). Ettinger was indeed a distinguished person, a professor of criminology at the Warsaw Free University.

Adler is careful to present the opinions of the adversaries as their own. He also considers every conversion opportunistic. But there is no reason to assume that Ettinger's conversion was opportunistic. We know that he was a member of the All Saints parish council (Czarnecki 1972, 207), a position rarely sought or attained by nominal Christians.[7] Adler's own feeling on the matter of the employment of converts on the *Judenrat* are to be found later in the same entry:

> The question of engaging baptized Jews for positions on the Jewish Council continued to be the theme of discussion not so much among the Jews of Mosaic belief as among the neophytes themselves. Within the Jewish Council's domain there was no animosity or antagonism directed toward baptized persons whose forced sojourn in the ghetto had bound them to the fate of the rest of the ghetto population; on the contrary, they provoked universal compassion for their difficult situation. As far as I know, baptized Jews never encountered obstacles in obtaining community [*Judenrat*] posts after the Quarter's borders were closed [November 1940]. The best proof of this is the fact that some of the most important posts were held by the neophytes. (1982, 170)

Adler goes on to list some of those important Christian officials: Colonel Józef Szeryński, head of the police, and some of his hand-picked assistants; Mieczysław Adam Ettinger; Ludwik Hirszfeld, chairman of the Health Council for

---

7. According to Marianowicz (1995, 49), Ettinger also organized clandestine law school courses in the ghetto.

infectious diseases, especially typhus; Dr. Mieczysław Kon, director of the Health Department; Major Dr. Tadeusz Ganz (Ganc), medical officer in the Polish army, commissioned to direct the battle against epidemics; Gomulicki (Gomuliński), director of the Supply Office; Czarnecki, one of the directors of the Fuel Commission; Dr. Jerzy Landau, director of the Health Center; Dr. Józef Stein, director of the Czyste Hospital; Dr. Wilhelm Szenwic, department head in the Czyste Hospital, and Dr. Stanisław Tylbor, deputy head of the general secretariat; "as well as a legion of lower positions occupied by the neophytes" (171).

Another matter on which Adler touches was the assistance converts received from the Catholic organization Caritas: "They were organized within Caritas near the parishes on Grzybowska and Leszno Streets and not infrequently complained of injustice and made demands for special treatment. The fact that they had the advantage of subsidies and other assistance rendered by Caritas, an institution which was able to distribute very nutritious and cheap soup as well as substantial monetary assistance, did not prevent them from requesting and obtaining help from various Jewish institutions" (171). But we have seen that Rev. Czarnecki—who undoubtedly would have liked to emphasize the importance of the aid offered by Caritas—speaks about its more modest dimensions.

Another memorialist was Henryk Bryskier, a chemist deported to Majdanek concentration camp during the Jewish uprising in the ghetto. He escaped from the camp and spent several months hiding in the eastern part of Warsaw (Praga). He was liberated by the Soviet army in September 1944 and became chief of the Department of Chemistry in the Ministry of Commerce and Industry of the new Communist Polish government. This brave man survived countless perils only to die from a heart attack in October 1945.

After his escape from Majdanek, while still in hiding, Bryskier wrote a memoir in Polish: "The Jews under the Swastika, or the Warsaw Ghetto" (1967–68). He offers precise information, some of which has already been mentioned here. He repeats the rumors about the convert priests, and the attempts to create a special ghetto for the converts, and so on. But he also mentions the activities of "an Old Catholic congregation on Żelazna Street."[8] Unless Bryskier is wrong, this means either members of the National Catholic Church or the specifically Polish religious dissidents known

---

8. Bryskier mentions Old Catholics on p. 127. Several passages, other than those cited here, of Bryskier's memoirs were included in Grynberg (2002).

as the Mariavites. Nothing is known about the presence of either of those groups in the ghetto. Incidentally, Mary Berg also mentions a "church on Żelazna Street" (1945, 119).

Bryskier left a quite sympathetic obituary notice for the Jewish Christians in Warsaw, stressing that the repugnance toward *mekheses* diminished considerably over time:

> Almost all of them [converts] belonged to the intelligentsia. They shared the fate of the other Jews, except those individuals who managed to escape from the ghetto. What happened to them outside the ghetto would become known only when we met after the War. The Jewish society before the War considered the baptized Jews as renegades and they repudiated them. Such aversion exists now, but only in the conservative [Orthodox] circles and it does not manifest itself externally. One can meet the neophytes at different levels of the social hierarchy, not to exclude the honor of belonging to the *Judenrat*. Whoever wears an armband is treated as a fellow sufferer. . . . Very recently the German authorities formally forbade the administration of holy baptism [within the ghetto], but it was still done for some time, because Christ did not declare the war against the Jews. (1967–68, 126–27)

The last sentence, in which I do not detect any irony, seems to me to be clearly written by a person sympathetic to the believing converts.

Ringelblum assigned one of the participants in the Oneg Shabbath activities to write a report on the assimilationists and neophytes. Marian Małowist (writing under the pseudonym of Władko, see chap. 2, n. 1) presents many of his leader's views on the *mekheses*, but after he becomes acquainted with a few individuals, he modifies his view of at least some of the converted. He begins by defining his subject from a distinctly Marxist point of view:

> I have combined the description of the condition of assimilationists and the new converts to Christianity. This I did on my own; but, as I see it with fullest justification, since these two classes used to be very closely related and tied to one another. This is a salient fact. They were tied through bonds of family; of social contact and associations; and of trade and industry. Both groups were heavily represented in heavy and semi-heavy industries, in commerce or finances, and also in scientific associations and liberal professions. On the Boards of the

large Limited Liability Companies, converts used to sit beside assimilationists. They used to support one another and keep one another's
company. (1986, 620)

Małowist gives a history of the situation before the war, underscoring the
fact that only rarely did the assimilationists and Christian Jews support the
cause of the Jewish people. As with most Jews writing in the ghetto, Małowist
presents baptism as a materialistic or sociopolitical choice. He simply does not
consider the question of religious belief. He mentions that when he worked
for the Jewish Students' Association, he entered the homes of the recently
converted and saw "pictures of the saints and icons of the Virgin . . . on walls"
(622). He viewed these, naturally enough, as signs of protection, rather than
expressions of faith or religious emotion.

Małowist classifies the assimilationists and neophytes according to their
attitude toward Jews. He stresses the fact—well known to those who lived
under the occupation—that the decent people behaved selflessly, the others
did not, that the good became better, and the bad, worse. He gives many examples but usually of bad behavior. Małowist speaks about the activities of
the two parishes with obvious irony:

> The moment the Ghetto was imposed, there came about a drawing
> together of the baptized, the assimilationists and the Jewish masses,
> which was a natural result of circumstances. The baptized orga-
> nized themselves in the "Charitas" [caritas,—charity], consisting of
> two sections, the one at All Saints Parish on Grzybów [Grzybowski
> Square], the other at the Most Holy Virgin Mary Parish on Leszno.
> Priests used to announce from the pulpit that they would never forget
> their brethren in Christ; and partly, they kept this promise. They es-
> tablished public kitchens, where lunches were being distributed, and
> loan funds; they also furnished flats on the church premises which
> were given to converts to live in. Through the mediation of priests,
> news from the Aryan quarter were [sic] reaching the converts. These
> kept in a tight group headed by a pre-war neophyte, a one-time dis-
> trict court judge. Many of them donated regularly for Jewish pur-
> poses. (1986, 626)

The former district judge mentioned by Małowist was probably Ludwik Lindenfeld, head of the Jewish prison on Gęsia Street. He was killed in August
1942. As for the Jewish charities, we must remember that the financing of the

ghetto social services, especially the soup kitchen, depended very much on voluntary contributions.

Although Małowist stresses the mercenary nature of conversions, he mentions meeting a real Christian, a Calvinist:

> An intelligent man, he used to speak in a judicious manner about the Christian idea. He used to invoke the example of the Gospel. He spoke of the motivation behind his conversion without denying that he never ceased being a Jew. He contended that Judaism had become warped and distorted which makes Jews practice their religion in a mechanical way. One has to carry one's God in the heart—he said—and not keep Him outside in the void. This he documented by mentioning the absence of commercial ethics on the part of Jewish merchants. Generally, these merchants were the target of a sharp reaction against Jews, on the part of converts and assimilationists. (1986, 626–27)

Małowist agrees with this negative appraisal of Jewish merchants, but points out that their behavior resulted from age-long persecutions. With obvious approval, he cites this Christian's doubts about the sincerity of his brothers.

But the next example he gives is not a good one. He describes the funeral of a Jewish Christian, the wife of a prominent doctor. Małowist attended the service in the Church of All Saints. A young priest (doubtless Rev. Antoni Czarnecki) performed the ceremony. Małowist was shocked because many took off their armbands in the church, and because not all of them knew how to behave during the funeral mass (Małowist 1986, 427). But of course a prominent doctor must have had many non-Christian friends (like Małowist) attending the funeral who would not know the behavior proper to mass (e.g., that one should kneel down at the Elevation, etc.). Nevertheless, he writes movingly about the end of the ceremony: "When the service was over, and Christian employees of the undertaker carried out the coffin to the motorcar hearse, a painful moment ensued—the family parting from the corpse. The authorities never allow the converts, whom they regard as Jews to leave the Ghetto. . . . [T]he priest and the sacristan, carrying the cross, took their seats and the family remained in the Ghetto. This scene will never leave my memory. It was genuinely tragic" (627–28).

Ringelbum also mentions such funerals in almost identical terms in his *Relations* (1992, 210). And there are other descriptions of Christian funerals in the ghetto. Antoni Marianowicz, a Christian belonging to the Reformed-

Evangelical church, describes, as we shall see, the funeral of his father. And Aron Koniński relates the funeral of a Jewish Christian from the Nativity parish: "The deceased was a baptized Jew, one of those strange oddities [*dziwolągi*] in the life of Jewish Warsaw. . . . The family of the deceased walked behind the casket with their armbands, and the Jews looked at them with irony and pity at this strange sight."[9]

Echoing other Jewish ghetto writers, Małowist reproaches the converts for "sticking together": "They are a group apart in the Ghetto. Many of them attend services, after which they obtain food. In the church they meet a few Christians, through whom they keep contact with the Aryan side. The situation of the poor among them has turned worse lately, for Charitas, evidently short of funds, cut down its activities and the soup for the converts is being issued out of the funds of the Jewish Self-Help Committee, therefore at the expense of the Jewish Community" (1986, 628).

Małowist insists that in the ghetto neither the *mekheses* nor the assimilationists changed their negative attitude toward the Jews and Jewishness. His last example is that of one of the most prominent among the *mekheses*, a famous medical scientist and cancer specialist. Without mentioning his name, Małowist speaks about Dr. Józef Stein, who was killed with his family in Treblinka in 1943. This "extreme assimilationist," whom Małowist had known since he was sixteen, "became baptized . . . not for sake of a career, but rather to sever ties with Jews, who always used to annoy him" (1986, 629). This respected professional—then heading the Jewish Orthodox Hospital on Czyste Street—and outstanding human being had become aware of many bad human characteristics in the Jewish medical world of the ghetto (intrigues, denunciations, etc.). They were absent, according to him, from the Polish medical milieu. Małowist agreed that these negative Jewish characteristics exist, but unlike the doctor, he ascribed them to the long history of persecution. His attitude toward the converts echos the traditional Jewish philosophical view by which one is a Jew irrespective of ideology. Thus he asked the doctor whether he would stay in his present position (obviously meaning "after the war"). "He said quite honestly that being a convert, he should feel bound by his ethics not to keep a paid position in a Jewish institution in normal times" (630). Małowist asked if he would return to the bosom of Judaism and offer his science to the service of the Jewish masses when the situation in Poland became better. The doctor answered that it was possible. Małowist concluded, "Such an individual should definitely be regained for Jewry" (630).

9. Archives of the ŻIH, Ring I, 282; see Leociak (1997, 624).

Winning back the assimilationists and the converts is, in fact, the main theme in Małowist's report, which, as noted above, does not take into account any religious element in the conversions. According to him, most of the persons who converted before the war did so for materialistic or professional reasons, and during the War in the false hope of not being classified as Jews. A minority of decent converts became Christians because they could not stand the Jews. It is significant that while strongly disapproving the majority, he seems to understand the minority.

Among the ghetto diarists there is one who, though he disapproves of the converts, is able to see *religious* reasons in conversion: Chaim Aron Kaplan. We have seen (in chap. 2) the nature and circumstances of the publication of his Hebrew-language diary. His first statement about the ghetto Christians appears in the entry for November 30, 1939, the day of the German decree obliging the Warsaw district Jews to wear an armband with the Star of David:

> The Nazis have marked us with the Jewish national colors, which is our pride. In this sense, we have been set apart from the Jews of Lodz, the city which has been annexed to the Reich. The "yellow badge" of medieval days has been stuck to them, but as for me, I shall wear my badge with personal satisfaction.
>
> I shall, however, have revenge on our "converts." I will laugh aloud at the sight of their tragedy. These poor creatures, whose number has increased radically in recent times, should have known that the "racial" laws do not differentiate between Jews who became Christians and those who retain their faith. Conversion brought but small deliverance. The conqueror was accustomed to ask the Jews seized for forced labor, *"Jude?"* The convert could of course "tell the truth" and say no. But now the conqueror will not ask, and the convert will not "tell the truth."
>
> This is the first time in my life that the feeling of vengeance has given me pleasure. (1999, 78–79)

Remembering, as I do, many Jewish converts to Christianity, I believe that these converts, whether sincere or not, had lost their Jewish traditions (or "faith" in Kaplan's words) well before their baptism. And having read Kaplan carefully, I do not really believe that this is the first (or last) time that he enjoyed his feelings of schadenfreude.

Throughout his diary, Kaplan is lucid and outspoken. And as a Jew and an observant Jew, he disapproves of conversions, but in contrast to his secularized brothers he also considers the religious aspect. Thus on January 9, 1941, three weeks after the ghetto was sealed off, he observes:

> All the churches inside the ghetto were closed and walled up, so that Aryan worshippers would not pass through the streets of the ghetto on their way to prayers. There is only one church, in Leszno Street near Solna [the Nativity of the B.V.M.; Kaplan apparently did not know the Church of All Saints] which although it is in an "unclean" area remains open, and there the Catholic Godhead continues to dwell. Its doors are wide open for all who seek the word of Jesus. It is always full of worshippers who pour forth their prayers before their Father in Heaven, the Son of God.
>
> But do you know who these pious Christians are? They are not Christians by race but Christians by conversion, people born in the Jewish race, whose souls thirsted for the "religion of love" but who remained inferior racially even after baptism. This is a truly unique tragicomedy, that Christians dedicated heart and soul to their faith wear the "badge of shame" on their right hand and the Holy Cross on their left. Even their priest is a Jew [here Kaplan repeats the false rumor concerning Rev. Puder] and although he is a priest of a noble deity he must nonetheless wear the "badge of shame." These Christians have no place in the Aryan quarter, since they are considered the same as Jews; so the conquerors assigned a special church for them inside the walls of the ghetto, and said to them: "Your Lord is a Jew also! So both of you go to the ghetto!" (1999, 237)

In reality, no Jewish Christian wore an armband with a cross on the left arm. Kaplan has perhaps repeated the rumors that mistook the Red Cross armbands worn by medical personnel for a religious sign. But even the Red Cross armbands were disallowed by the Germans early in the Jewish quarter's existence.

I also wish to remind the reader that Kaplan's gloating tone must be accepted as given. He never minced words on any subject. He was hard on the *Judenrat*, on its representatives, on the Zionists, and he was particularly hard on Jews in general. See his entry for January 4, 1942:

The words of a poet have come true in all their dreadful meaning: "'Tis not a nation nor a sect but a herd." Gone is the spirit of Jewish brotherhood. The words "compassionate, modest, charitable" no longer apply to us. The ghetto beggars who stretch out their hand to us with the plea: "Jewish hearts, have pity!" realize that the once tender hearts have become like rocks. Our tragedy is the senselessness of it all. Our suffering is inflicted on us because we are Jews, while the real meaning of Jewishness has disappeared from our lives. (1999, 289)

Kaplan often speaks like a modern and lucid Jeremiah. Five weeks before the *Aktion* many people still doubted the reality of the impending destruction of the Warsaw Jews (doubts cleverly encouraged by Nazi lies), but Kaplan saw clearly, on June 16, 1942, that "the process of physical destruction of Polish Jewry has already begun, but it is possible that Warsaw will be the last. When the Führer announced [in 1939] to all the world that the Jewish race would be eliminated from Europe, we said, 'He is only tormenting us. It would never happen.' . . . Now this is no longer a prophecy for the future, but a terrifying horrible reality" (351).

Kaplan did not cherish the apostates, especially the recent ones. His diary entry of March 7, 1941, concerning the converts is analytic but characteristically bitter:

Since the time of defeat there have been many apostates among the Jews. For people educated in a foreign culture there is no reason for these tortures. Why should they risk their lives for something that is strange to them? Ossified Judaism did not furnish them with the strength necessary to continue their national lives, and even though they knew in advance that race would still be a handicap for them, it did not prevent them from taking the formal step of leaving Judaism. Even if they were not accepted into the foreign milieu at once, they would be after a while, when their entrance was forgotten — especially since priests were found who arranged not only the religious aspect but the racial aspects as well. Just as money purifies bastards, it purified the children of a foreign race. After the priest received a certain sum in cash, he simply wrote a birth certificate stating that so-and-so is an Aryan from a long line of Aryans. These certificates are assumed to be genuine and no one disputes their veracity. Those who knew such things say that "proper certificates" of this sort have been given to hundreds and thousands. The priests made fortunes, and these impoverished members of Polish Jewry enjoy all the rights to which the Aryan race entitles its offspring. They remained outside the ghetto area legally and are treated as genuine Aryans. (1999, 249–50)

Kaplan, to be sure, is wrong to stress purely mercenary motives on the part of the priests or the ease with which they could grant a false certificate. Locked in the ghetto, he had, like most of the ghetto dwellers, only vague ideas about the real situation on the "Other Side." At the beginning of the war, some of these false certificates were made for the parishes beyond the Bug River, that is to say, in Soviet-occupied Poland, but this procedure became unsafe after June 1941. All the inhabitants of the GG were required at that time to obtain the new identity card (*Kennkarte*). To prove one's identity, a baptismal certificate—which served as a birth certificate—was necessary. Since the Germans could easily verify a baptismal certificate and would, if fraud were discovered, execute both the priest and the certificate seeker, the priests had to be very careful. They could offer certificates only to those whom they could trust. Usually they would search in the parish registry of deaths for a person whose birth date roughly corresponded to the birth date of the certificate seeker, and then issue a baptismal certificate bearing the name of the deceased. Ewa Kurek (1997), who studied all aspects of rescuing Jewish orphans, believes that the Nazis never realized that they should have examined these parish registries of deaths in order to verify the baptismal certificates. Thus Kaplan's description of granting baptismal certificates is inaccurate. A large cash payment to a greedy priest could not by itself procure a certificate of undisputed "authenticity."

Kaplan continues to discuss the fate of the descendants of the converts in his entry for March 7, 1941:

Above this group was another category of "Jews," those who were born into Christianity. They were born to apostate parents, and so they don't have the slightest feeling for Judaism, either religiously or racially. But the conquerors checked and rechecked, and the family secrets were discovered. Maybe Jewish informers who were jealous of these Christians' peaceful existence were involved, or perhaps some Pole tipped the Nazis off about irregularities in the family trees of their coreligionists. At all events, the conquerors began a hunt for these *Pans* [*Pan* is a Polish word for 'gentleman'] who originated from the Jewish race and who, in their [Nazis'] eyes, are considered Jews in every respect. The Nazis brought a great caravan of them to the ghetto and turned them over to the president, Czerniakow, who was stunned to see them in their ruin. He had known them as the cream of Polish society, people who always showed their hatred for the Jews and who adhered closely to the customs they had adopted. Some of them are descendants of financial and industrial titans, and some of Polish litterateurs, but neither wealth nor knowledge nor genealogy was of any consequence. Like members of the rabble caught in crime and sentenced to severe punishments, they were led back to the ghetto before the eyes of passersby among the ghetto dwellers. Huge crowds accompanied them to the gates of the *Judenrat*. Like unclean people who have no place in human society, they were removed suddenly from the environment in which they had been born and raised.

Who of them imagined that his origin was in the ghetto? Who of them dreamed that his ancestor stood on Mount Sinai? The good-for-nothing Czerniakow took them into his office with a great show of respect and commiserated with them. I cannot sympathize with their tribulations. One fate for all.[10] I don't doubt that Czerniakow's heart bleeds for them, but fate has made him a leader in Israel, and it doesn't behoove him to spread his wing over apostates and the sons of apostates.

I don't know what their end will be, but one thing I know for a certainty. Their enmity to Israel will never cease. (1999, 250)

This sad passage, obviously written by a man in pain, requires some comments. First, not all descendants of converts were classified as "Jews" as a result of Jewish or Polish denunciations. Given the date of this entry, Kaplan doubtless speaks here about the "Ronikiers." Many of them bore distinctly Jewish names and were not, therefore, hiding their provenance. When they acknowledged their origin (in December 1939), they did not realize the consequences of their disclosures. Hardly anyone could foresee the horrors to come. Second, other Jewish diarists, as we have seen, stressed that the *mekheses* received favorable treatment from the *Judenrat* and its *Obmann*. But

---

10. Here Kaplan echoes a common ghetto cry "Ale glakh!" made popular by the singing of a well-known and slightly insane street jester, Abraham Rubinsztajn: ('Shabes far ale yidelakh / urem, rakh, ale glakh" ('Sabbath for all the Jews / Poor, rich, all [are] equal').

I have argued that if they were favored, it was not because they were Christians, but because they possessed many administrative and scientific skills lacking among the majority. Third, the belief that Jewish converts to Christianity are particularly virulent "enemies of Israel" is based on a historical tradition. Ever since the Middle Ages and as late as the eighteenth century, certain neophytes participated in anti-Judaistic polemics, sometimes citing the virulently anti-Christian passages of the *Talmud* (without mentioning the parts containing universal ethical messages). Kaplan, a traditional Hebrew scholar, was doubtless aware of these polemics.[11]

Kaplan's last statement about Jewish Christians comes on April 6, 1942. I quote it because it expresses clearly Kaplan's struggle with the definition of a Jew:

> A sensational development took place this week. Under the supervision of Nazi guards 2,600 Jewish citizens of Germany were delivered to the outskirts of the ghetto. Their reception as Jewish evacuees from Germany is what made the event so remarkable. People are saying that the Gestapo and the Poles welcomed them at the railroad station with food and flowers. . . . It appears that they [Germans] will build a ghetto within the ghetto for them.
>
> But who are these people? In racial terminology they are half-Jews. Many of them were born into the Christian faith, their parents or grandparents having converted years ago. Many were children of mixed marriages. Some of the wives are pure German. In other words, in practice they are Christians in every way, full-fledged Germans, who before 1933 occupied important positions in all the professions. What is ironic, is that they despised the Jews as much as the Germans do. If their birth certificates had not betrayed them, they would be more Nazi than the Nazi themselves. Their problem was that anyone tainted with Jewish blood unto the third generation is forbidden to live among the Nazis. Nazi law defines them as half-Jewish. (1999, 309)

Many German Jews, Christians or non-Christians, were, indeed, brought to the Warsaw ghetto on several occasions. Czerniaków mentions that 1,000 were expelled from Hannover, Gelsenkirchen, and other places on April 1, 1942, and 1,025 from Berlin on April 5, 1942 (1999, 339, 341). The historian

---

11. On this attitude of the converts in the specifically Polish historical situation, see Kulik (2003).

Marian Fuks also states that in the Warsaw ghetto "there were a certain number of Protestants, among them the most prominent were German Jews, whose number reached several thousand. Some of them came to the ghetto together with their non-Jewish German wives, who did not want to separate themselves from their unfortunate husbands" (1999, 66). Kaplan's particular interpretation of the fate of the German Jews and half-Jews in Warsaw undoubtedly had its source in the innumerable rumors and exaggerations continually arising in the *Zwangsgesellschaft* of the ghetto. The ability of the ghetto to generate rumors, often optimistic ones to counterbalance the dreadful reality, was jokingly known in the ghetto as the Giraffe Agency, (*Żyrafa* = *ŻY*dowska *R*Adosna *FA*ntazja, or "Jewish Joyful Fantasy"). In the spring of 1942 no other diarist mentions a "ghetto within a ghetto" for the German Jews. Ringelblum, however, as early as December 10, 1940, repeats the rumors that: "the converts are to have a ghetto of their own within the larger ghetto" (1958, 105–6). We know now that there were no plans for a special ghetto for the German Jews or German *mischlinge*.

That Poles welcomed the newcomers from Germany with food and flowers was also a rumor based on the natural but wishful belief that life on the "Other Side" was normal, that is, closely resembling prewar times. In April 1942 no Pole would have welcomed any German (*mischling* or not) with food and flowers, and even if he had wanted to do so, the *Herrenvolk* would not have permitted him. It is clear that Kaplan does not consider those German refugees as Jewish, and that here he is repeating the widespread opinion that former Jews and their descendants are more anti-Semitic than other persons.

Dr. Henryk Makower, a secularized and quite assimilated Jew, was a protégé and a good friend of Dr. Hirszfeld. He was quite sympathetic to the converts—not to converts in general but, as we shall see, to the group of converts from the parish of All Saints. An outstanding member of the medical profession, Makower collaborated in teaching medical courses in the ghetto (he taught physiology). In the Berson-Bauman Hospital he was the head of the ward for infectious diseases. He escaped from the ghetto with his wife, Naomi, also a doctor, on January 24, 1943. Like Hirszfeld, Makower also wrote a book in Polish, entitled *Memoirs from the Warsaw Ghetto: October 1940–January 1943* (1987) while in hiding on the "Other Side" in 1943, and like Hirszfeld, he died a normal death, of heart disease, on March 11, 1964. His wife published his work more than half a century after the events depicted: "I cannot escape the feeling," she says in the preface, "that my husband wished to get rid of the ghetto experiences in order to be able to lead again a normal life as a physician" (1987, 5). Makower was the personal physician of the chief of the Jewish police and in that capacity he encountered many important ghetto personalities. His book, published in the twilight of the Communist regime, was not translated into any Western European language. It is an important document, especially for the history of the *Judenrat*.

Incidentally, Makower offers a curious detail concerning Nazi propaganda and All Saints Church: "The church was partially destroyed in September [1939], and several buildings surrounding it lay in ruins. Somebody told me that in a German propaganda film, he saw Grzybowski Square presented as a part of destroyed London" (1987, 180).

Makower's commentary about the expectations of those who were being transported to Treblinka, made by such a well-informed member of the ghetto community, must be taken seriously: "I write those words exactly one year after the beginning of the 'Resettlement' of the Jews from the Warsaw ghetto. We used the word 'Resettlement' then. We supposed, at that time, that it was indeed a resettlement, even if it was barbaric and horrible (15 kilograms of luggage, 100–200 people to a cattle car), but not extermination. Now [July 1943] it appears to me very strange that we deceived ourselves for such a long time" (1987, 205). There is really nothing strange in this self-deception. First, the Germans were very clever at deceiving people about their real intentions. The solemn denials of rumors of annihilation and letters from the deported mailed in the eastern territories are well known. Second, the transported refused to believe in the "final solution" because no human being, and especially no group of human beings, can easily and willingly accept the idea of its total extermination. Just as the Shoah in general baffles the imagination, so too the destruction of the Warsaw ghetto dwellers went beyond anything they could believe in the days of the *Aktion*. Makower was a witness of the last hours of the parish of All Saints. We shall see his testimony in the next chapter.

Considering the voices of the ghetto dwellers expressed in the above testimonies, one obvious conclusion may be drawn: they demonstrate a broad range of opinions and attitudes. This realization should serve as a warning against easy generalizations about the "Jewish viewpoint." Perhaps the only possible generalization concerns the date of composition. The diarists who wrote before the *Aktion* and the final destruction of the ghetto were exasperated with the ultimate assimilationists. Those who, like Ernest, Bryskier, and Makower, wrote after May 1942, however, are far less inclined to voice disapproval or scorn the converts. A common fate and common feeling of dread of the present and future assuaged the initial feelings of antipathy. *Ale glakh!*

The last voice is that of Jechiel Górny, who wrote a very sympathetic account of the Christian Jews. According to Ruta Sakowska (1993, 162, 232), Górny was one of the most faithful collaborators of the Oneg Shabbath archives, copying (one original and two carbon copies) many dozens of documents. The theme that Ringelblum assigned to this fellow member of the Left Po'alei Zion Party was the "destruction of Warsaw" (*hurbn Varshe*). Górny survived the *Aktion* and wrote an account of the second deportation in January 1943. He fought in the uprising and died on May 10, 1943, trying to reach the "Aryan" side through the sewers.

Górny's report, written in Yiddish sometime in June 1942, does not dwell on any traditional Jewish consideration of Jewishness and apostasy. Endowed with considerable literary talent, Górny simply draws a picture. He offers a passing glance at a group of the ghetto Christians which, while underscoring their exotic strangeness, is filled with sympathy, commiseration, and an overwhelming sense of nostalgia for a lost normal life. I offer here my translation (from the Polish version) of the whole passage referring to Jewish Christians:

> Sunday, June 14, 1942, 9 p.m. . . . Through the open window we hear the sound of the church organ. There must be a service in the church on Leszno Street [the Nativity of the B.V.M.], whose small garden is adjacent to our apartment house on 23 Nowolipie Street.
>
> How precious is the view of a few trees in bloom, of plowed earth and green grass in the overcrowded ghetto!
>
> After about 15 minutes the voices of the choir reach my ears. I finish my meal quickly and come to the window.
>
> Groups of people in their Sunday best walk the paths of the church garden. Gentlemen in dark suits, ladies in elegant summer dresses. Among them, I see a tall person in black cassock with his hands folded on his back—the priest. The conversations must be very joyful—from time to time laughter clearly reaches me.
>
> But the laughter does not last. The organ music ceases. The walkers sit down on the benches and chairs probably set up expressly for this special evening.
>
> As if following an order, every sound disappears only to reappear again as a marvelous choir sings to the organ accompaniment. Quietly, slowly and then a little louder the tones of a religious hymn rise in the air. The priest, sitting in the middle, leads the singing and those gathered—or perhaps a special choir—continue their hymn.

It is getting darker and darker. First the people's forms, then the faces disappear in the descending night. And then—what irony!— only the patches on their right arm, the white armbands with the Star of Zion, are visible.

Fate had it that those who for all sorts of reasons had parted company with the Jews either themselves, or through their fathers or grandfathers, were thrown back to their original place by the creators of the 20th-century barbarism. Many of them, especially the young, did not even know that their ancestors were Jews.

There is a more elaborate ceremony tonight in the church. It must be a wedding.

Thrown behind the walls, separated from their Aryan kin, it seems that the converts do not wish to forget their adherence to the Catholic Church.

The hymns slowly cease. With difficulty, I can recognize "God who for centuries" sung in soft voices. The spirit of patriotism—the spirit of liberation from the yoke of Hitlerism—is alive everywhere.

Thus ends the religious service of the converts in 1942, in the 20th century. (1942, 33–34)[12]

The nineteenth-century religious and patriotic hymn "God who for centuries" ("Boże coś Polskę")—a prayer for the restoration of country and freedom— had to be sung sotto voce, since both the words and the melody were forbidden by the occupier. The evening service described here was permissible because sometime before the *Aktion* the curfew was extended from 9:00 p.m. to 10:00 p.m.

But, exactly thirty-nine days from that Sunday the *Aktion* would begin, and—unless they managed in the last moment to find a shelter on the "Other Side"—all those elegant ladies and gentlemen would share the lot of their brothers, first in the *Umschlagplatz* and then in Treblinka.

The spirit in which Jechiel Górny describes the converts did not die. Ruta Sakowska cites his magnanimous words at the end of her short section on the Christians in the ghetto (1993, 139–40), and it was she, I believe, who had translated this particular passage from Yiddish to Polish. There is no doubt in my mind that this learned and generous historian shares Górny's sentiments.

---

12. Górny's account can be found in the archives of the ŻIH. I thank the personnel of the ŻIH for supplying me with a Xerox copy of this document.

CHAPTER SIX

Christian Voices

Some time ago, a friend of mine invited me to see a short film made recently for Polish television about the All Saints parish (Dobrzański 1995). The film begins with a short history of the church. The building itself is a depository of precious historical memories. The church and Grzybowski Square were famous for the 1905 anticzarist demonstrations. The building was damaged in 1939, half-destroyed in 1942, and completely destroyed in 1944, its ruins defended heroically during the Polish uprising in August and September. The body of film consists of present-day pastor Monsignor Zdzisław Król's interview of one of the former residents of the parish building at All Saints, Dr. Louis Christophe Zaleski-Zamenhof, who now lives in France. He is the grandson of Dr. Ludwik Lazar Zamenhof (1859–1917), the creator of Esperanto; the main street of what used to be the northern ghetto bears his name. Dr. Zaleski-Zamenhof is the honorary president of the International Esperanto Union.

When he was fifteen, Zaleski-Zamenhof lived in the ghetto with his mother, who had just been released from Pawiak prison. His mother was a widow; her husband had been executed in Palmiry (a forest near Warsaw, the site of numerous executions carried out by the Gestapo), at the beginning of the occupation. Her sister, a medical doctor and also a recent widow, lived with them. They were invited to live in the All Saints parish hall by the pastor, Rev. Godlewski. Later, the pastor helped the young Zamenhof to escape from the ghetto and to find a humble factory job in suburban Anin. The chief reason for making the film was to observe the fiftieth anniversary of the death of the Reverend Marceli Godlewski (1865–Dec. 26, 1945).

In the film, Dr. Zaleski-Zamenhof speaks in glowing terms of Rev. Godlewski. He does not consider him an anti-Semite: "He did not ask me what was my religion, but whether I was hungry." On the contrary, he maintains that even from a purely theological point of view, the ideas propagated by Rev. Godlewski in the Warsaw ghetto were forerunners of the new ecumenical view, later accepted by Vatican II, that Jews are not the "rejecters of Christ" but "the older brothers of the Christians." The film begins and ends with Dr. Zaleski-Zamenhof placing two roses, one red and one white, on Rev. Godlewski's grave. This simple but moving testimony, as well as my exchange of letters with Dr. Zaleski-Zamenhof, encouraged me further in undertaking the present book.

———

The Jewish Christians in the Warsaw ghetto probably did not have as many diarists as did the Jews, or if they had, few of their writings survived. I shall return to the situation of the surviving Jewish Christians in my last chapter. We do have important testimony concerning the parish of the Nativity of the B.V.M. Alina Brodzka Wald, a University of Warsaw professor, remembers the parish very well. She has graciously answered my inquiries and has written to me about her childhood memories. She lived in the ghetto between November 10, 1940, and July 22, 1942. She was twelve years old when she escaped to the "Other Side." Brodzka Wald gives a very *personal* explanation for the reluctance of Jewish Christians to write about their ghetto experiences, but I believe that this explanation might well apply to other Christian Jews who survived the ghetto: "Do you understand why I did not write my memoirs? Because I consider myself to be an undeserving [*bezprawne*, lit. "unlawful," "illicit"] child of good fortune. I have received nothing but kindness from people. Who am I to speak about the Shoah? I do, of course, speak about the Shoah—I do not hide my past experiences. But I have received the grace and the good fortune to be always with good people. No blackmailer [*szmalcownik*] was ever on my trail." We must ponder this reflection carefully.

This is Alina's ghetto story. She was baptized early in her life, following her mother's wishes. Her godfather was Stanisław Wiesel (or Wizel), a convert of long standing. In 1942 he made it possible to place little Alina in an orphanage run by the Sisters of the Family of Mary, an institution well known for saving many "non-Aryan" children. Alina's parents went to the ghetto in November 1940 because of their deep attachment to their own parents, who were old and had refused to go into hiding, although they could have done so because their Polish was fluent and faultless. Salomon and Gustawa Brodzki died peacefully in the ghetto, before the *Aktion,* "therefore our moving to the ghetto made sense." One of Alina's aunts, Eugenia Brodzka Jakubowicz, was baptized in the ghetto "at the time that there was nothing left to do but die—and she did die." As a little girl, Alina felt the antipathy of the ghetto population: "We were not loved, we were strangers."

Alina left the ghetto on the first day of the *Aktion,* July 22, 1942. She simply walked through the checkpoint with slightly falsified papers, in which the Jewish name Brodzka was modified to the more "Aryan" spelling Brocka. But nobody asked her for papers. She explains it as a combination of luck, youth, and her "Slavic" looks. We must remember that escaping from the ghetto was not as difficult as staying on the "Other Side."

Alina's first protector was Jadwiga Bielecka, the wife of a well-known "Endek" who was at that time a prisoner of war in Germany. Alina spent the rest of the German occupation with the Sisters of the Family of Mary, and then with the Sisters of the Resurrection in Warsaw. After the Polish uprising, during which this fourteen-year-old girl worked in a hospital, Alina was sent with the Sisters to Częstochowa in the western part of Poland. Both Alina's parents survived on the "Other Side." Her older brother, who left the ghetto well before her, was an active AK member and took part in the Polish uprising.

The day that Alina's family arrived in the ghetto her father took her to the Church of the Nativity of the B.V.M. For the next almost twenty months, she went to the parish every day to attend the school, taught by priests as well as lay teachers. She remembers the horror of those trips. Daily life in the ghetto was rendered particularly difficult because, among other things, of the incredibly crowded conditions in the streets. One especially dreaded street was the narrow Karmelicka, the only passage, until the fall of 1941, from the southern part (small ghetto) to the northern part (larger ghetto). Alina had to take this passage to reach the church on Leszno Street from her home on Orla Street. Ringelblum writes about "the crowds on Karmelicka Street [which] are impossible to describe. On the sidewalks and pavement flow constant, compact waves of people. Getting through is an incredibly difficult and a time-consuming job" (1988a, 196; quite different in Ringelblum 1958, 86). This Karmelicka Street passage was called "Gibraltar" or the "Death Canyon," because Germans, either placed there or driving by in their cars to reach Pawiak prison, used to beat the crowded passersby (see Leociak 1997, 63–64).

For Alina, entering the small door into the church garden, after the horrors of Leszno and Karmelicka Streets, was like entering another world, a world of green nature, one of tranquillity and a sense of security. She knew the head of the parish, Monsignor Popławski, Rev. Teofil Głowacki, and Rev. Zyberk-Plater, whom she remembers as the "intellectuals of the parish." Alina belonged to the parish children's group, which had several dozen members. The leader of this group was the Rev. Henryk Komorowski, the priest whom Alina remembers best. He played volleyball with "his" children, and Alina's most cherished souvenir that she managed to bring from the ghetto is a photograph of the parish volleyball team dedicated to her by Rev. Komorowski as "his dear player." He was a truly charismatic person, not only respected but loved. He enjoyed the total trust of his wards.

The school offered the usual subjects as well as a course of studies in the Christian tradition. Besides sports, the parish offered dancing and rhythmic gymnastics lessons given by Irena Prusicka. The parish had run an elementary school from the inception of the ghetto. At first it was a clandestine enterprise, but in October 1941 it became a legal Catholic school. Regular religious education was offered both in the school and outside it.

We know that the gardens of both the Nativity and All Saints churches were greatly admired, desired, and envied as the only islands of green in the sea of overcrowded and noisy streets. The Nativity parish garden was more substantial than the garden of All Saints or the deactivated Saint Augustine. As Jachiel Górny describes it (quoted in chap. 5), the elite among the converts used to meet in the garden of the Nativity Church: doctors, professors, engineers, and teachers. The garden was rented by an engineer and his wife, who, among other things, cultivated flowers which they sold. Miriam Eisenberg, who worked in the garden from the spring of 1942 until the *Aktion*, mentions the garden and remembers that she was "enchanted with the green, with the flowers, and with the quiet atmosphere jarringly different [*drażniąco różna*] from the atmosphere of the streets."[1] We shall see similar reactions from other Christians who were in the ghetto.

Alina Brodzka Wald's story parallels that of a young Protestant man who also spent about twenty-two months in the Warsaw ghetto. Antoni Marianowicz (original name: Kazimierz Jerzy Berman) left a memoir, *The Strictly Prohibited Life* (1995). Despite my considerable efforts to unearth documents treating the lives of non-Catholic Jewish Christians, *The Strictly Prohibited Life* is the sole testimony I found concerning Protestants in the Warsaw ghetto. This

---

1. I base my description of the Nativity parish on Mrs. Brodzka Wald's personal communication as well as on her recorded statement published by Engelking and Leociak (2001, 622). The authors mention there that Miriam Eisenberg left her statement in Jerusalem (Archives of Yad Vashem, document O3/2196).

book, as well as another autobiographical work,[2] was written many years after the war. It is composed as a series of loosely organized reminiscences that treat much more than his life in the ghetto. An important and recurring thread is Polish-Jewish relations, particularly after the fateful year of 1968, when the Polish Communists launched a general "anti-Zionist," that is, anti-Semitic, campaign. Marianowicz is a serious journalist and writer. He began his career as a journalist with the satirical weekly *Szpilki*. He has published poetry, children's literature, poetry translations, and studies of Jewish life.

Antoni was slightly older than Alina. He was about seventeen years old when he came to the ghetto in October of 1940. He begins the recollections of his life in the ghetto with an attempt to define his origins:

> I was never a Jew in a religious sense. My family left the Mosaic faith many years ago, and I was baptized immediately after my birth by the Superintendent of the Reformed-Evangelical church, Rev. Władysław Semadeni. I am not a neophyte, for I have never changed religion. . . . I am not religious, but I am happy to belong to the Reformed-Evangelical Community, for I have received many instances of Christian charity from that Community. I consider myself a Christian, for, to put it simply, Christian ethics appeals to me more than any other ideology. This consideration is based on a strictly personal choice. (1995, 13)

For a long time, Marianowicz remained quite indifferent to his origins: "I was quite ignorant about Jewish culture, since my family broke all its contacts with that culture. I did not know Yiddish because for the last three generations our family did not use it. I ignored the significance of Jewish feasts, Jewish faith, and Jewish customs. My ignorance was much greater than that of young Poles growing up in the neighborhoods with many Jews. I grew up in the heart of Warsaw, where only the assimilated Jews lived" (1995, 16–17). Even after his stay in the ghetto and after dangerous years of hiding on the "Other Side," Antoni was not very conscious of his origins. After the war he kept his assumed name, chiefly because (Jakub) Berman was the name of one

---

2. *Poland, Jews and Cyclists* (1999). This book contains frequent comments on the reception of and the problems raised by *The Strictly Prohibited Life*. Its whimsical-sounding title refers to a well-known German joke from the 1930s: A person who complains about the situation in Germany is told, "It's all the fault of the cyclists and the Jews." He asks, "Why the cyclists?" and receives the answer, "Why the Jews?"

of the two most important and the most hated Stalinists in postwar Poland. While never hiding his origins, he became fully conscious of them only after the 1968 anti-Jewish campaign. He wrote *The Strictly Prohibited Life* as an old man fully aware of his Christian faith, his Jewish origins, and the meaning of both in contemporary Poland.

Antoni's family could have tried to avoid moving to the ghetto: "We could very well have stayed hidden on the 'Other Side.' We had the so-called 'good looks,' which in the language of the time of the Occupation meant the lack of distinctive Jewish features. My mother's looks could be described as excellent, mine as very good, and my father's as merely good. We spoke flawless Polish, we did not gesticulate while speaking, and as Christians we were completely conversant with the customary behavior of Polish society. Furthermore we had many friends, among whom at least half were ready to help us" (1995, 45). It must be said that Antoni's father was quite rich, and that made the move into the ghetto much less painful. The chief reason for moving there was his father's health. He suffered from a serious heart condition (angina pectoris) and required a quiet life and uninterrupted medical care. He was well known in Warsaw, and hiding under a false identity, with all the daily stresses of illegality, was beyond his strength. The young Antoni simply could not think of separating from his father at that juncture.

But there were other reasons for the family to declare themselves Jewish and to go to the ghetto: "Our decision was also influenced by our illusions about the Germans' intentions. The fact of going to the ghetto was a legal solution, and the Germans were known then for their respect for the law. We believed that it would be better to live according to their rules and regulations" (1995, 136).

Once in the ghetto, the young Antoni got a job with the directorate of the Provisioning Authority (Zakład Zaopatrywania). He thus had good papers protecting him from being drafted for forced labor and, later, the "Resettlement." The family lived in the Sienna Street district, which we have seen described by Jewish writers as the "Converts Avenue" and an "island of peace" in the ghetto.

Antoni was nostalgic for his former life and describes his feelings in a moving way:

I remember . . . a scene which had a symbolic meaning for me: Leszno Street was crowded with a moving throng of hungry, desperate people, mad from fear and condemned to annihilation. Right above them, [I saw] the balcony of the Reformed-Evangelical church, which, although it was outside the ghetto, formed a real enclave into its territory. On the balcony stood Rev. [Stefan] Skierski. He looked at the crowd with an indescribable expression of horror and compassion. I wanted to make a sign to him, to let him know that I saw him. But it was hopeless—from the height of the balcony he could not distinguish individuals, he saw only a human swarm. But his presence was a sign for me that there, on the "Other Side," was somebody who thought about us, who watched. It was a sign that I would find friends there who would help me to survive. (1995, 86)

The death of his father was precipitated by a typical ghetto "accident." On the October, 4, 1941, Antoni was walking home through the infamous "Gibraltar" passage into the southern part of the ghetto. He was preoccupied with thoughts of the impending diminishing of the ghetto, as the Sienna Street district was to be cut off. (In fact the new border would run down the middle of Sienna Street, the northern side of the street still remaining in the ghetto.) A young German stood on Leszno Street receiving "homage" from the Jewish passersby. Preoccupied by his thoughts, Antoni forgot to take off his cap and bow down to the German, who leaped toward him, threw down his cap and gave him two or three sharp three blows on the face, breaking his glasses. Antoni was stunned and covered with blood. He ran home in that state, not stopping to wash his face. When his father saw him he said softly, "I will not live through this" (1995, 276). Indeed, he suffered a massive heart attack that very night. Antoni blamed himself for his father's death.

Antoni describes the difficulties in obtaining a permit for the burial and, above all, permission to leave the ghetto territory to attend the funeral in the Reformed-Evangelical cemetery, adjacent to the ghetto. The permit was obtained through the good offices of the Reformed-Evangelical church and the Polish commissar-president of Warsaw, Julian Kulski, but only for Antoni and his mother. His two uncles and aunt could not accompany them. Antoni's reactions to the brief excursion out of the ghetto to the funeral were typical:

After the lengthy checking of the documents we got into the car. My mother and I left the ghetto for the first time in a year. The trip was short, the streets seemed to me empty and quiet. At the cemetery I was struck by the soothing peace and the phenomenon of vegetation. In the ghetto, we missed the greenery so much that even the

October landscape of the cemetery seemed to me a paradise, and the funeral seemed an escape from the land of stony death to the land of ever-regenerating natural life.

We had notified only a small number of friends about the funeral, but there was a nice crowd of people, among them some who risked [their lives] by their presence [they were the Jews in hiding]. I was happy to see my Aunt Konarska. We knew that she was living under her own name, but with false ["Aryan"] documents. (1995, 280)

At the funeral, a friend of the family proposed a safe place on the "Other Side" for Antoni and his mother. They could not accept it immediately, because the church officials had given their word to Kulski that both of them would return to the ghetto. But they would accept this offer some nine months later.

Antoni's last memory of the short excursion into the "land of the living" is the reaction of the children nearby: "When we were returning to the car, wearing our armbands, children on Żytnia Street pointed their fingers at us and whispered: 'Look, the Jews!' There was no animosity in their voices, only curiosity in seeing the officially branded people. I think that as the 'incendiaries of the world' [the usual Nazi description of the Jews] we presented a rather sorry sight" (1995, 281).

Like Alina, Antoni and his mother escaped from the ghetto at the beginning of the *Aktion*, on July 29, 1942. Their immediate reason for fleeing was the Provisioning Authority's order that Antoni, as an employee of the Provisioning Authority, would have to assist the Jewish Order Service in rounding up people for the "Resettlement." Antoni could not bring himself to do it. Thus he lost his job and, more important, his "life-protecting" employment certificate.

Antoni describes the escape from the ghetto in some detail. It had been prepared in advance. Antoni and his mother received "good" false identity cards, and armed with these documents they left the ghetto through the Municipal Court building on Leszno Street, which heard both Jewish and "Aryan" cases. They entered as Jews through the Jewish entrance and met the judge—involved in their plans to escape—who had summoned them to his office. There, they took off their armbands and, in the company of several lawyers whom the guards knew, left through the "Aryan" exit showing their "good" papers. The rest of *The Strictly Prohibited Life* deals with Marianowicz's complicated and dangerous existence during the war on the "Other Side."

The reminiscences of Dr. Zaleski-Zamenhof, Alina Brodzka Wald, and Antoni Marianowicz furnish many details of the atmosphere of the Warsaw ghetto as seen by young Jewish Christians. Their memories are centered on their respective parishes: Dr. Zaleski-Zamenhof remembers the All Saints Church; Alina, the Nativity of the B.V.M.; and Antoni his lost Reformed-Evangelical church, visible but not accessible from the ghetto.

The All Saints Church was situated in the southern part of the ghetto, sometimes referred to as the small ghetto. Some details about the parish life at All Saints can be found in the short and cautious article by Rev. Antoni Czarnecki (1981) described in chapter 2. He gives some of the names of those who lived in the parish hall. Besides Professor Ludwik Hirszfeld and his wife and daughter, there were Rudolf Hermelin (engineer) and his family, Polakiewicz (lawyer) and his family, Feliks Drutowski (engineer) with his mother and sister, Zygmunt Pfau and his wife (Bronisława) and daughter, Dr. Fedorowski and his parents, Dr. Gelbard (later known as Gadomski), the Grynbergs, the Zamenhofs, and others. Tadeusz Bednarczyk (1995, 135) adds two names: (Henryk) Nowogródzki, a lawyer, and Dr. Jakub Weinkiper-Antonowicz.

Rev. Czarnecki remembers that many people who were moved into the ghetto found homes by exchanging apartments in the vicinity of All Saints, "so that . . . a considerable part of the population there was constituted by Catholics or Christians of other denominations, or of sympathizers with the Church. The great majority of the new parishioners belonged to the intelligentsia: they were scientists, doctors, artists and lawyers" (1981, 207). Given this membership, the parish council naturally included members of the intelligentsia and "outstanding personalities such as Dr. Antonowicz, Dr. Górecki, Dr. Grausam, the lawyer Ettinger, the engineer Hermelin, Mrs. Bronisława Pfau and others" (207).

Dr. Ludwik Hirszfeld lived in the parish hall of the All Saints Church, and thus we know a little more about this church than about the Leszno Street parish (the Nativity of the B.V.M.). Given that communication from the southern to the northern part of the ghetto was difficult, some Jewish writers (e.g., Chaim Kaplan) knew only about one or the other church.

Dr. Ludwik Hirszfeld is the most knowledgeable informant about the Christians in the ghetto and about many aspects of the daily life of the ghetto dwellers. His autobiography, *The Story of a Life* (2000) is the most important document by a Christian about the Christians of the Warsaw ghetto and about the Church of All Saints. Unlike the journal of Emanuel Ringelblum, Hirszfeld's *Historia* is a fully fledged autobiography, written in 1943 and 1944 when he was living in hiding.

Hirszfeld begins with his student years, his discovery of his love of science, and his life in Heidelberg and Zurich as an assistant and a young scientist. His heroic times were during World War I, when he participated in the medical campaign against typhus, first in the Serbian army and then in the Allied "Armée d'Orient" based in Salonika. His wife, Hanna Kasman, accompanied him as a medical doctor and a researcher. Their beautiful and only daughter, Marysia, died from tuberculosis after their escape from the ghetto. Hirszfeld writes about his research, his attendance at many international congresses, and his university career in Poland between 1920 and 1939.

All this ended in September 1939, when the German army entered the defeated Warsaw. Hirszfeld cites the German scientific reviews praising his research only to add sadly: "Ten years later Germans removed me from the Institute, because of my belonging to the 'parasite race'" (2000, 153).

Hirszfeld devotes nine chapters to his life in the ghetto. Because he lived in the rectory of All Saints Church, his observations and impressions are crucial for our purposes. Even if Hirszfeld had not treated the subject of Christians and their church, his memoirs would be an important document for the history of the Warsaw ghetto in general. Given that he was working as the medical head of the antityphus section, he was in a better position than many others to know the truly dreadful health conditions prevailing in the ghetto.

Cruelly disappointed and shocked by the German treatment of those who did not consider themselves Jews, the "Ronikiers," he entered the ghetto convinced of the deadly intentions of the Nazis, and when he wrote he was fully aware of the extent of the *Aktion* and the total destruction of the ghetto. His first chapter on the ghetto, "The City of Death" ("Miasto śmierci"), begins as follows: "Once upon a time, the Turks decided to get rid of all the dogs in Istanbul. Their customs forbade killing animals. Therefore they sent the dogs to an uninhabited island, so they could devour each other. This way of getting rid of the dogs was considered cruel and unworthy [of humans]. But that was then. Now the Germans decided to destroy the Jews. They were to die of hunger, lice, and dirt, or—like the Istanbul dogs—they were to devour each other" (2000, 277).

Hirszfeld writes like a scientist, but one endowed with a strong moral sense. His postghetto chapters, written immediately after the Soviet army entered his village on August 18, 1944, contain profound reflections on anti-Semitism and nationalism. Hirszfeld is frank and honest about these matters. He also discusses the organization of medical and scientific training, the sanctity of the scientific calling, social problems, and his absolute condemnation of Nazi science.

Hirszfeld does not speak about his early youth and does not mention his own conversion. The closest he comes to mentioning his religious background is in the opening paragraph of his chapter on the Jewish *nation* in Poland. He analyzes the question of separateness and assimilation, elucidating why Jewish writers in the ghetto speak about the assimilationists and the converts in the same breath. Here is the opening paragraph of his chapter, significantly entitled "The Turning Point of the Jewish Nation" ("Punkt zwrotny narodu żydowskiego"):

> My destiny has been strange. I come from a totally assimilated [*zasy-milowana*] family, I spent my life in the company of liberal [*postępowi*] Poles and assimilated Jews, and I have never discovered any essential difference between these two. Next, I lived for a year and half in the greatest concentration of Jews in the world, at a time when they were forced to organize something like their own state. And then I lived as an authentic Aryan in an aristocratic conservative milieu of landowners. All sorts of problems which I had never fully appreciated appeared to me in all their complexity. The problems of the Eastern Jews had formerly always seemed to me to be very similar to the problems of the Jews in the West, where the Jews had wished to join the nations among whom they had lived. They did not wish to become a separate nation [*naród*], only a separate religious community. (2000, 488)

The chapter is a discussion of Jewishness in general in the face of nationalism everywhere, but in a sense it is also an examination of the author's conscience. This examination permits us to surmise how this naturally religious man—he even speaks about science in religious terms—became a Christian. The chapter concludes:

> The Jews [in Poland], or rather the small group that survived, face the following alternative: either become completely like the others or emigrate and create their own country. Both decisions should be respected and both require the work of several generations. May those who are making the choice now know that he who merely continues [his existence] is not noble and happy, his happiness is the happiness of a weed; only the one who strives is happy. All living things wish to become the beginning of a new life. But all that is noble wishes to bear fruit. Let everyone, therefore, look deeply in his

heart and make a decision: *homeland here or homeland over there.* (2000, 501)

In the ghetto Hirszfeld learned that he himself belonged to the "homeland here," but also that there has always been a Jewish nation or a Jewish people: the Polish word *naród*, which he systematically uses, incorporates both concepts. Hirszfeld pays tribute to the Jewish nation in his moving chapter "The Last Effort of a Perishing Nation" ("Ostatni zryw ginącego narodu") (452–62). It is one of the earliest and most moving homages to the heroes of the ghetto uprising, one that understands fully all the moral meaning of the gesture of armed resistance. It is written in the form of excerpts taken from an underground booklet "In the Eyes of the World" ("Na oczach świata"). In 1944 Hirszfeld thought that the booklet was composed by the fighting organizations of the ghetto. We now know that it was in fact written by Maria Kann expressly for the Bureau of Information and Propaganda of the AK.

Hirszfeld's story of his stay in the ghetto must necessarily begin with his "Ronikier" status (2000, 274). In order to understand why Hirszfeld, and many other prominent Jewish Christians, went to the RGO and asked for "clarification" of their status by the German authorities, we must remember that in their minds they were not Jewish but members of the Christian confessional community, the only term used before the German occupation to define their identities. They believed that their parents and grandparents were certainly not members of the "Mosaic religious community." They went to the RGO because they were used to respecting the law and, as rather conservative people, they were, like the Marianowiczes, not yet aware that Hitler's Germany was no longer the land of the harsh but law-observing Germans which Poland remembered from its 1915–18 occupation. Hirszfeld was German educated and he knew the best of Germany—the Germany of Heidelberg. He assumed that the permit to stay outside the ghetto issued by the German medical authorities would be respected. At the same time, he believed the RGO's announcement that Christians of "non-Aryan" origin who belonged to the families who had contributed to the social life of Poland might be released from the obligation to wear an armband. Hirszfeld applied and received the permit because of his prewar scientific activities and because of his uncle, Bolesław Hirszfeld's prominent position in educational and political life.

In August 1940, when they were still living outside the Jewish quarter, the Hirszfelds decided to emigrate to Yugoslavia. The representative of the

Yugoslav consular service was most friendly and assured Hirszfeld that, because of his services during World War I, he would be well received in that country. The real possibility of reaching Yugoslavia existed until the German invasion of that country on March 27, 1941. It was also possible to reach the United States until Hitler's declaration of war, December 9, 1941. After that date—except for individuals for whom a heavy ransom was paid by American friends—the only people who had a chance to leave German-controlled Europe were persons, like Mary Berg, having some claim on American or Allied citizenship who could be exchanged for Germans held by the Allies. As soon as Hirszfeld's Yugoslav friends learned about his difficult situation, they persuaded the king to sign honorary citizenship papers for him and his family. The RGO extended his "Ronikier" status immediately. Later Hirszfeld came to believe that this status was a trap and that the RGO authorities gave, perhaps unwittingly, the list of persons who had received the permit to the Germans. We know now that the list was, in all probability, handed to the Gestapo by a collaborator inside the Warsaw RGO office (see chap. 3, n. 2). Hirszfeld and his family were allowed to live in their own house outside the ghetto while they were waiting for the German exit permit. Only in February 1941— that is, even before the outbreak of the German-Yugoslav war—was he told that he had not received the permit and had to go to the ghetto.

Hirszfeld had to leave all his possessions behind, and most of the meager personal effects that he was able to bring were stolen by German policemen at the gate of the ghetto. Seeing a book written in German by Hirszfeld, a policeman asked who wrote it: "I did," answered Hirszfeld, "when I was an employee in a German institution." Whereupon the policeman observed, "Jetzt bist du aber nur ein Jud [But now you are only a Jew]" (2000, 275).

Hirszfeld was profoundly shocked by his new environment. He offers his thoughts in the chapter entitled "The City of Death":

> I am now one of the crowd of the unfortunate, and so are my wife and my daughter. Only recently, we walked in the Park of the Pasteur Institute in Gareches, and we rested on the bench once occupied by Pasteur himself. I was proudly thinking then that, thanks to my past efforts, I was making it possible for my daughter to reach the summit of scientific achievements accessible to great minds [Marysia began her medical studies in 1938 in France]. And instead I led this child to Grzybowski Square. Poor child! I brought her up in the Polish traditions, I taught her to love that country. And now a foreigner has chased us out of our home and told us that we have no right to

walk on Polish soil. And now I see that my daughter can grasp neither where she is, nor what the new world wants of her. (2000, 287)

Slowly the first shock passed and Hirszfeld realized that he had an obligation to help the ghetto dwellers. He understood the difficulties of the undertaking well. He describes his obligations in clearly religious terms: "I did not know the Jews, and I was not sure whether I would reach their hearts. But after all, I did manage to reach the Serbian souls. Doubtless the values of the soul are eternal. Psychology of races—let us leave this nonsense to the Germans. By a religion of love we may reach the hearts of the unfortunates. If a new slogan 'Unfortunates of the World Unite,' were to be realized now, the Jews would be the most numerous among them" (2000, 289). Since Hirszfeld considered training in a scientific discipline the highest form of a *religious* education, he concludes, "[My students] felt that they were indeed pariahs. But when I met them, I realized that they needed a priestly care" (289). He also believed that his personal scientific authority would influence the Occupier, whose antityphus campaign "was worse than the epidemic itself" (289). Hirszfeld made a decision: "If I can go abroad, I will. Over there, I will fight on a larger plane and for my people. But if I cannot, I shall not leave the quarter and I shall not go into hiding. I do not want future generations and my own conscience to say to me: 'Fate has put you together with several hundred thousand unfortunate people, what have you done for them? You have received from destiny a key to open young hearts. Have you tried to open and to console those poor hearts?' (290).

Thus he decided to stay, although his friends on the "Aryan" side sent "good" identification papers for him and his family and urged them to go into hiding: "I stayed on despite the fact that I had nothing: neither influence, nor means, nor laboratory. I was a foreigner to that people. As a Christian I was rejected by the crowd. I had, however, a boundless sense of compassion. This was my only capital and my only weapon" (290). Next he had to decide whether the family should separate: "I said to my wife: 'I must stay, but you should take our daughter and leave this hell with her. In the country she might get well again.' I saw in my wife a struggle between the mother's and companion's instinct. And I saw that the companion's instinct won. We turned to our daughter: 'My dear, we have friends who wish to save you. And it would be easier for us if you were on the "Other Side." ' But our daughter was made of good stuff . . . : 'I will be where you are.' And thus all three of us remained together in hell (290).

As an important medical specialist, Hirszfeld met the head of the *Judenrat*, Czerniaków. Hirszfeld offers us a sympathetic portrait of this tragic figure, probably one of the earliest of such portraits.[3] Since Czerniaków has been such an object of debate, and since Hirszfeld's book is not available in the West, let me quote the relevent portion:

> Superficially, the Chairman gave an impression of hardness. He was tall, stout and his advanced jaw made him look a little like Mussolini. He wished to appear hard, but he was endowed with the soft heart of a man who felt that he was condemned, and wished to offer himself as a sacrifice. He fought to the last moment. A great portrait of Piłsudski decorated his office in the *Judenrat*. He never removed this emblem and symbol of Polish statehood. Some time ago the SS-men arrested him. He was badly beaten, and released after a few days. He came straight to his office with his face still marked by the blows. Across from his office was an empty place left by a bombed-out building. He arranged for a playground there. When he was tired, he looked at the children playing: the view gave him strength for further work. He supported learning and the arts. He was accused of spending funds on unimportant things, when these funds could be used to support the refugees. But he had a tough-minded approach to life, and he maintained that the spirit makes people live, and that since he could not save everyone, he wished to save those who represented the future. This was the reason he supported children, artists, and scholars. (291–92)

Hirszfeld's activities during his next year and a half in the ghetto were of two kinds: he offered Czerniaków his services as an expert on combating typhus, and he participated in organizing and offering important courses for medical practitioners (doctors, pharmacists, and dentists) and also collaborated in a semiclandestine course for medical students which was officially called the "Course of Sanitary Preparedness for Combating the Epidemic" but in fact was a program of the first two years in medical school. The chief

---

3. The only earlier and also basically sympathetic portrait that I have found is the sketch drawn by Stefan Ernest (2003, 150–53). Ernest stresses the impossible position in which Czerniaków was placed, as well as his disinterestedness, goodwill, and spirit of sacrifice. Ernest's only reproach is that the *Obmann* was not a man to actively resist.

organizer of this course was Professor Juliusz Zweibaum. Hirszfeld taught together with professors Mieczysław Centnerszwer, Hilary Laks, Henryk Makower, and others (Sakowska 1993, 119–21). As on the "Other Side," the Germans, afraid of epidemics, allowed some basic retraining courses for doctors and for auxiliary medical personnel. But what matters most to us here are Hirszfeld's thoughts about his educational activities. His motivation was frankly spiritual and, as we have seen, often expressed in a clearly religious language. And this language is maintained throughout his discussion of his work in the ghetto.

His first lecture for medical practitioners met with some resistance because of his *mekhes* status: "The Chairman [Czerniaków] is present, evidently to prevent any demonstration against me by the Jewish nationalists. At the door a woman doctor, a nationalist, urges the boycott of my lecture. . . . My first words are a call to maintain dignity. Our enemy wishes to deprive us, Poles and Jews, of everything that represents science or art. It is possible that we shall perish, but let us perish with dignity" (2000, 295). But he succeeded in gaining his audience: "These people hanker for meetings, for exchange of thought, for anything that brings to their minds the better, prewar, existence" (296). The printed prospectus for further courses bore this motto: "Learning—my hope and my consolation."

An even more "pastoral" tone can be seen in Hirszfeld's description of his younger students: "I see above their heads the halo of future martyrdom. I am convinced that I must above all keep up their spirits. Often they look like small frightened birds. I look at their faces and I realize that not many will survive, for the power of hatred is too great. Should I speak to these condemned about bacteria, should I examine them in bacteriology? No, I shall take them in a great sweep of thought, I shall offer them a consolation by appealing to a strong Jewish virtue, their hunger for learning" (2000, 298). From the lecture room close to the ghetto wall, amid the noises, the cries, the shots fired by policemen, Hirszfeld led his "children" to a better world: "Look, I used to say, I am with you behind the Wall, any ruffian can kill me or any one of you at a whim. But, because of my love of science, I can travel in my thought to far away countries. . . . And thus, I took those poor children by the hand and led them to the summit where the air is pure, where the people pray ecstatically at sunset, and where nobody would hold them in contempt. And, surrounded by the halo of human dignity, they will be able to build, to think, and to dream" (298).

Hirszfeld realized very quickly that a victim of racism sequestered in inhuman conditions, deprived and persecuted, tends to acquire a sense of his own inferiority and feels, in the words of the German policeman, that he is "only a Jew": "I decided right under German eyes to discuss the most forbidden subject, the subject of racism. I wanted to remove the curse of contempt from these young people, since it is easier to suffer hatred than contempt. I did not want these young people to die with the feeling that they deserved to die. I realized that if anyone denounced me to the [German] authorities I would lose my head. But I counted on my power over their souls" (2000, 299). In fact, Hirszfeld received many manifestations of enormous gratitude for his educational work, which in turn encouraged him to further efforts and kept up his own spirits. There is reason to believe that Hirszfeld correctly understood the feelings of his students. For example, in his deposition written after the war, Dr. Juliusz Zweibaum states that "the attitude of the students to their studies was very serious, almost religious."[4] Hirszfeld's chapter "Lectures and Courses," from which I am quoting here, also describes the scientific work done in the ghetto and contains some tributes, including obituary notices of several of his colleagues.

The chapter "Typhus in the Quarter" offers further elucidation of Jewish attitudes toward his Christianity. Czerniaków encountered some resistance when he appointed Hirszfeld chief of the Health Council for combating typhus, but after a while, as with his teachings, his professional expertise won out over the objections. Hirszfeld quotes Izaak Ajzyk Ekerman, a member of the *Judenrat* from the Orthodox party, as saying that he "did not care that I was not a Jew: 'When one is sick, one goes to the professor without asking about his religion'" (2000, 321). More weighty were the objections of his wife, Hanna:

> I turned to my wife for advice. She advised me against [taking the job]. Speaking above all as a loving wife, she maintained: "The struggle against the epidemics is wrought with bribes. They will cover you with mud and say that you profited from the tragedy. The Jewish nationalists will say that you are trying to shove yourself into their midst, and the Polish nationalists will say that you must have been convinced that you were a Jew, since you went so far in collaborating with them. In the end, you will remain alone and your scientific work will suffer. Take care of yourself for the sake of your scientific work and for our sake." (321)

---

4. Archives of the ŻIH, document no. 4108, cited by Sakowska (1993, 120).

But Hirszfeld thought differently: "Through a strange accident tens of thousands of human beings have placed their trust in me. When they learn that I am trying to fight the epidemics, they will perhaps sleep better at night" (321). Hanna Hirszfeld was right in a sense, for one of Hirszfeld's acquaintances accused him of collaborating with the Germans by taking a position in the Health Council (322)! As a member of the council, he met other Jewish Christians, for example, the already mentioned and very gifted Dr. Józef Stein, "who was a Christian and considered himself Polish" (324). He comments on the gradual acceptance of the Jewish Christians: "Right after the creation of the quarter, Jewish nationalism did not allow the Poles of Jewish origin to take any official positions. But the composition of the Health Department and the Health Council can stand as a proof that this period ended quickly, for there as in other domains, one encountered Jewish Christians" (324–25).

For our purposes, it is interesting to note two points: First, Hirszfeld invariably speaks about the Jews as "they." And second, he systematically uses the term "nationalists" to describe various Zionists as well as Polish anti-Semites.

As a Christian Jew—or a Pole of Jewish origin, as he sometimes describes himself—he presents his opinions concerning Polish anti-Semitism with his usual optimism, although optimism was not easy to maintain in the fall of 1943 while hiding in the Polish countryside. He notes that during his earlier professional visit to the ghetto prison on the Gęsia Street, wearing his armband, he was told by some Jewish prisoners that they had received help on the "Aryan" side. He expressed joy:

My nation accused by the world of anti-Semitism is a good nation. [It gives assistance] despite the death sentence for the help, and despite the inherited antipathy toward Jews. I believe that if Jehovah maintains the register of all the injuries suffered by Jews, he will erase the Przytyk pogrom,[5] university disturbances, and separate seating for Jews [in the universities], because Polish antipathy lasted only as long as there was a vision of powerful Jews. It was replaced by pity when the pauper appeared. It was the case during the Jewish martyrdom. (2000, 350)

5. On March 9, 1936, a pogrom took place in Przytyk near Radom in which three Jews were killed. One of the pogromists was also killed, by a Jew acting in self-defense. The court denied obliquely the Jews' right to self-defense, for it condemned eleven Jews and twenty-five non-Jews for the disturbance. See Ringelblum (1992, 12).

But wisely Hirszfeld adds immediately: "Naturally there were other facts, which I shall treat later."

Hirszfeld's hopeful, if not wishful, views of anti-Semitism were doubtless a typical result of the wartime atmosphere. In the midst of the horrors of German occupation, there was a strong tendency in the ghetto (and on the "Other Side") to see the real problems of prewar life in a somewhat more positive light. I remember a typical ghetto joke that illustrates this: Two elderly Jews meet in the ghetto early in the morning. The first says "I had a marvelous dream: I was walking on a street in Warsaw and I saw the signs: Boycott the Jewish stores! Send them to Palestine! etc." "So what was so beautiful about this dream?" asks the second Jew. "Our people [the Polish administration] were back!"

In the chapter entitled "In the Shadow of the All Saints Church," Hirszfeld describes Jewish Christian life in the ghetto. In August 1941 the Hirszfelds obtained living quarters at All Saints in the large church building containing the rectory and a church hall. After almost seven months of living on Twarda Street, in the midst of noise and filth and with constant exposure to the terrible street scenes, they found themselves in an oasis of relative peace. Hirszfeld describes this new place in terms similar to those Alina Brodzka Wald used about the Church of the Nativity of the B.V.M.: "The windows of our very small dwelling were facing a small but beautiful garden. These gardens surrounded by walls have a strange charm. We had an impression of finding ourselves in a recess of meditation, silence and goodwill, a recess preserved in the midst of hell. And the priest of this recess was Monsignor Godlewski" (2000, 361).

Hirszfeld praises Rev. Godlewski in the highest terms. We have already seen the same homage offered by another survivor of the rectory of All Saints, Dr. Zaleski-Zamenhof. Hirszfeld, who insisted that he was not endowed with literary talent, always speaks lyrically about the monsignor. He refers to the prewar economic and social anti-Semitism of Rev. Godlewski: "Monsignor Godlewski. When I pronounce this name, I am seized with emotion. Passion and love dwelling in one soul. Once upon a time he was an anti-Semite fighting in spoken and written words. But when fate made him encounter bottomless misery, he abandoned his previous attitudes and turned all the ardor of his priestly heart toward helping the Jews" (2000, 361–62). As we have seen, Rev. Godlewski was an "Endek," or member of the National Democratic Party. His very large and mostly poor parish population lived side by side with Jews who were also mostly poor. Any help to the struggling Polish artisans, small shopkeepers, and house servants automatically clashed with the interests of the Jewish artisans, shopkeepers, and employers of servants. The line between competition and conflict was very thin. Hirszfeld does not go into explanations because he knew perfectly well that there was, and still is, a large range of meaning to the term "anti-Semite."

Hirszfeld says that his admiration for the pastor of the All Saints parish was shared by many: "Whenever his beautiful white-haired head . . . appeared, the other heads bowed in admiration and love. We all loved him: children or old people fought for a moment of conversation. He did not spare himself. He taught catechism to the children. He was the head of Caritas for the whole ghetto, and ordered that soup be given whether the hungry person was a Christian or a Jew" (2000, 362). Hirszfeld insists that this love and respect was shared by people outside the Jewish Christian group as well: "We [Christian Jews] were not alone in the appreciation of Rev. Godlewski. I would like to transmit to future generations the opinion of the Head of the Jewish Council [Czerniaków]. During a meeting that Dr. [Juliusz] Zweibaum called to observe the first anniversary of the medical courses, the Head of the Council told us how this Monsignor wept in his office when he spoke about the misery of the Jews, and how he tried to alleviate this misery. Czerniaków stressed the great assistance rendered by this former anti-Semite" (362).

Rev. Godlewski lived in Anin, a nearby suburb of Warsaw, and commuted to the ghetto every day using a permanent pass. His relative freedom of movement was extremely important for making contacts, for smuggling small quantities of food and medicine, and, according to a well-established tradition, for smuggling out little children hidden in the fold of his large cassock.[6] His assistant and second in command at All Saints was, as we know, a much younger Rev. Czarnecki, who lived permanently in the rectory and who apparently was not touched by prewar anti-Semitism. Hirszfeld speaks about him also in high terms: "The helper and deputy of the Monsignor was Rev. Antoni Czarnecki. He was a young priest, who did not have the same passionate approach to life as the Monsignor, but he was certainly endowed with a gentleness and goodness worthy of a priest. He was liked and respected by all. His pleasant and loving ways [sposób bycia] had a soothing and comforting effect" (362).

This chapter is the only one in which Hirszfeld speaks about the Christian Jews as a group: "On Sunday all the Christians, not only the Catholics, attended Mass. Everybody was there: doctors, lawyers, those whose baptism

---

6. See Bednarczyk (1995, 135). Bednarczyk was an active AK member, in the unit specializing in giving assistance to the Jews. He offers precious information concerning false baptismal documents furnished by various Roman Catholic parishes.

was an expression of faith, those for whom it was a [Polish] national symbol, and those who, at a certain moment, accepted their baptism to further their own self-interests. But all felt the need to gather at least once a week in the church and to participate in the service" (2000, 362–63).

Here too Hirszfeld speaks directly about his own faith, although as a scientist he was obviously unaccustomed to disclosing his intimate feelings: "My life there was strange. I have never had as close a contact with the Church as I did in the Jewish quarter. For the whole year, every day, morning and evening, I breathed the atmosphere of the church silence, and I frequented the people whose profession was the mission of goodness" (362). But Hirszfeld was not alone in his faith: "[During the services] I noticed a large number of not only believing but practicing Christians [i.e., those taking communion]. Even the daily mass was attended by a number of faithful. In wintertime, the penetrating chill of the damaged church did not keep them away. The church services for those sealed off behind the Wall was a unique experience" (363).

Hirszfeld attempts to present, albeit in slightly abstract terms, the religious experiences that he doubtless shared with many of his fellow Christians in 1941 and 1942:

> Gloria in excelsis Deo. Glory to God in the highest and peace and goodwill to men. Grzybowski Square and Twarda Street disappear. The excited and feverish crowd of the poor also disappears. We are immersed in the coolness and atmosphere of the place of worship. There is a throng of us there lost in prayers. We can no longer see the killers and the haters—we are in the company of the enraptured [skupieni]. We are united in a sentiment of higher communion.
>
> Agnus Dei—embodiment of goodness and of healing contact with the infinitely good Being. We do not have to be ashamed of our ugliness—after all, the soul ceases to be ugly at this moment, [it reaches] a soothing starry coolness of celestial spaces. Our sufferings, our enemies and our hideous disgust at the very thought of mankind—[at the thought of] a man who has ceased to be a man. All this disappears as in a fog. The infinite space becomes real, the worlds float on, guided by the laws of eternal mind and goodness. (2000, 363)

I should explain that these two paragraphs are a meditation on two phrases of the mass. The Gloria, "Glory to God," is said in the first part of the Sunday and holiday liturgy. It is a prayer of praise to the Creator. The Agnus Dei, "Lamb of God who takes away the sins of the world," is a prayer that introduces the last part of the mass, the communion. What follows next is Hirszfeld's meditation on the phrase of the Lord's Prayer "Forgive us our trespasses as we forgive those who trespassed against us," recited just before communion. This passage is presented as a question asked of God, followed by God's answer:

> "What is wrong with you my son?—Why should I love those monstrous men?—For no reason. Love is a state of the spirit. Everybody possesses it, but sometimes in a dimmed and muffled state. But it is as much an instinct as the hunger for life, as the joy of living. Love is a delight as much as a rapture amid the starry silence and the transport of joy of the dancing stars. There are no small things here—everything emanates from the Spirit." A heavenly music is heard. And in this harmony the soul bends down sobbing in humiliation. And it embraces the world in rapture, it floats in oblivion. Horrible people, horrible things disappear: all resonates with the Great Harmony. (363)

The mass is over: "We end the service and return to earth, but our souls have been invigorated by the coolness of the life-giving sources" (364).

These passages are followed by less mystical ones. The first is about sermons. (Its place is logical here if we remember that in the pre–Vatican II Polish churches the sermon frequently took place after the regular mass.) Hirszfeld's religious expressions do not employ intellectually and theologically powerful arguments. When he talks about Rev. Godlewski's preaching, he agrees with Marian Małowist's opinion that Christianization was a logical consequence of assimilation. He and presumably many of his fellow Christians, all of them belonging to and attending the services at All Saints, were not touched by a sermon on the child Jesus, or the idea that the road to the Son leads through his Mother, for such subjects were, says Hirszfeld, too much "attached to earthly things" (2000, 364). What mattered was the idea of religion as the binding element of the nation:

> [The congregation] was moved by the sermons on Poland. Monsignor Godlewski preached on this subject with beauty and courage. The country, the homeland, he said, is like a Mother. Sometimes she does us harm, sometimes in passion she becomes unjust, but we for-

give our Mother because she wishes nothing except good for her children. And he said that love of this Mother-Homeland is a power to bind the nation together. It is greater than a common [ethnic] origin. We gain our homeland by common, binding love. And our suffering makes sense, for it leads to higher aspirations. These were approximately the words of Rev. Godlewski. And these words were a balm for the disdained. (364)

There follow Hirszfeld's final reflections about his fellow Christians and especially new Christians who received baptisms in the ghetto:

There were many people who were baptized in the quarter—old and young, sometimes whole families. Some of my students were among them, men and women, and I was often asked to be their godfather. What motives drove them to the baptism? They never received any benefits from it. The change of faith did not entail any change in their legal status. No, they were attracted to it by the appeal of a religion of love. They were attracted by the religion of the nation to which they felt they belonged. They were attracted to the religion in which there is no room, or at least there should not be any room, for hate. Jews are so weary of the atmosphere of universal antipathy. Antipathy for what reasons? (2000, 364)

Hirszfeld's reflections contradict the views of those Jewish writers who saw in the ghetto baptisms nothing but a search for some kind of material profit. To concretize his reflections, he offers a specific example of a recent baptism:

Standing ready for baptism is my student. She has a Semitic nose and thick lips. I see in her eyes a deep longing for human sympathy, a sympathy which she wishes to repay from the fullness of her heart. Strong men will come, those who occupied the higher social strata, those priests of the new religion. They will take the little Jewish girl [Żydóweczka] by the hand and they will protect her from hate, they will allow her to be good. After all, Christianity became powerful when it extended the rights of equality and human dignity to those who suffered and were disdained. Equality before God and perhaps . . . before men. For it is terribly painful to live with the undeserved mark of Cain. And only a religion of love can and should remove this mark. Such were probably the thoughts that animated this girl when she was being baptized. (2000, 364–65)

These pages, which Hirszfeld wrote probably in the summer of 1943, present a strong argument that it is imprudent to offer any simplified explanation for the process of becoming a Christian, since there are many grounds for this process. What struck me in reading these pages for the first time—many years ago—was the insistence on patriotism, on an inalienable union of God and Country. I remember that during the war in Poland this was precisely the common, accepted, and indisputable view.

Hirszfeld is one of the witnesses of the closing of the two parishes of the Warsaw ghetto: "An order soon came to close both churches and to hand over the keys to the Germans. I remember the moment when Rev. Czarnecki came to tell us this dreaded Job's news. We had the impression that a chasm had opened before us" (2000, 386). Perhaps symbolic in his mind was the last event he remembered taking place in the parish of All Saints—another baptism:

> My friend, a young lawyer Tadeusz Endelman, had desired to be baptized for some time. In view of the coming threat of death, he asked [the priest] to arrange the rites quickly. Rev. Czarnecki did not refuse this last consolation. After the baptism, the priest went before the altar and began to pray. There was a small group of parishioners present. They all felt that this moment was a farewell to life. They all wept. Afterward, Rev. Czarnecki bade farewell to all the families in the parish hall. He encouraged them. At that moment, I arrived from town. He bade me good-bye with his eyes full of tears. He made a sign of the cross over me and went away. (386)

We should understand that Rev. Czarnecki agreed to baptize Tadeusz Endelman on the principle *in articulo mortis,* for normally in both parishes in the ghetto the baptism of an adult required several weeks of preparatory courses.

Rev. Czarnecki himself wrote about the last Sunday mass and last moments at All Saints. The scene described by Hirszfeld must have taken place after the mass, since the rite of baptism did not take place during mass in the pre–Vatican II church. Monsignor Godlewski could not come from Anin because his pass to enter the ghetto had been revoked some time before. Rev. Czarnecki, however, as a person living in the ghetto, still had a pass and could reenter. In July 1942 Rev. Czarnecki stayed in the country but returned just before the *Aktion.* He remembers his last day at All Saints:

Here is my last day in the ghetto and the last Sunday mass in the church: There was an enormous crowd, such as had never before seen in the church. I started the holy mass without singing and without organ music. I read the gospel according to St. Luke (19:41–44) prescribed for the ninth Sunday after Pentecost: "As [Jesus] drew near and came in sight of the city he shed tears over it and said, 'If you had only recognized on this day the way of peace! But in fact it is hidden from your eyes! Yes, a time is coming when your enemies will raise fortifications all round you, when they will encircle you and hem you in on every side; they will dash you and the children inside your walls to the ground; they will leave not one stone standing on another within you,—because you did not recognise the moment of your visitation.'" I read this vision of the destruction of Jerusalem with great difficulty. There was so much crying and clamor in the church that I did not need to preach a homily, even if I could. Jesus himself had spoken personally, movingly, and powerfully. (Czarnecki, 1981, 211)[7]

Rev. Czarnecki's statement gives us an exact date. In 1942 the ninth Sunday after Pentecost fell on July 26.[8] The farewells at All Saints described by Hirszfeld took place on Monday, July 27, 1942, following the last mass in the church: "The next day, Monday, I said good-bye to all the inhabitants of the Parish Hall, I blessed those gathered in the church. I removed the Blessed Sacrament to deposit it in the chapel at Sienna Street. Having bidden farewell to all those who lived in the shadow of the Church of All Saints, I left. Such fragmentary reminiscences cannot possibly reflect even a very slight part of the reality, which will resound in history with thousands of echoes" (Czarnecki 1973, 211–12). It is clear that the Hirszfelds must have left the ghetto and gone into hiding in the first days of the *Aktion*. Hirszfeld is quite laconic here: "It was the last moment. The very next day, the assassins came to the rectory. They sent everyone to the transport [to Treblinka], except those few who had killed themselves beforehand" (2000, 406).

Hirszfeld speaks with gratitude about the help he received in his escape. He and his family first received a place in one of the workshops, which temporarily protected them from the *Umschlagplatz,* then one of his former

7. I cite the biblical text according to the Jerusalem Bible, Standard Edition.

8. I wish to thank Rev. Kazimierz Rulka, of the diocesan Seminary of Włocławek (Poland), for verifying this date for me.

students from the "Other Side" invited them and supplied the funds necessary to transport them to the Polish countryside. Hirszfeld's reaction is typical: "My real love for the youth had probably lived on in the memory of this
friendly man. I accepted the proposal with the deepest emotion" (2000, 405).
The Hirszfelds left the ghetto in a column of ghetto laborers working on the
"Aryan" side.

Hirszfeld does not indicate the date of the destruction of All Saints,
but according to Dr. Zaleski-Zamenhof, the parishioners of the church went
to the *Umschlagplatz* on August 6, 1942. He remembers that it happened
at the same time as the transportation to Treblinka of Dr. Korczak and his
orphans. Like Henryk Makower, whose memoirs were cited in chapter 5, he
believes that most of the people did not know that they were going to an
extermination camp. On the contrary, many thought that they were going
to a labor camp where the conditions might perhaps be better than in the
ghetto.

Makower's memoirs contain a further testimony about the last moments
of the All Saints parishioners. This Jewish friend of the parish offers the following reminiscence:

> I was often a guest at the rectory, where Prof. Ludwik Hirszfeld and
> his family moved in the summer of 1941. I heard many good things
> about Rev. Godlewski, one of the two ghetto [All Saints] priests. In
> the first day [days] of the *Aktion* they were ordered to leave the
> church and their flock. Early in the *Aktion,* Germans and Ukraini-
> ans "fixed up" [destroyed] the rectory. They took all the inhabitants
> who did not manage to get to the "Aryan" side. From the windows
> of my hospital on Leszno Street I saw a great mass of people going
> from the small ghetto through Żelazna and Nowolipie streets to the
> *Umschlagplatz.* They walked in silence. All I heard was the sound of
> their shoes against the pavement. I noticed many of my friends from
> the rectory among these people. (1987, 180)

It is not surprising that Makower, like Henryk Bryskier (1967–68), presents
a sympathetic memory of his Christian friends. By the summer of 1942, most
of the aversion to the *mekheses,* especially among the educated and assimilated Jews, was probably quite forgotten. After all, by then they were sharing
the march to the *Umschlagplatz,* the march to Treblinka, the march to death,
together with their Jewish kin: *Ale glakh!*

As for the people of the ghetto parish of the Nativity of B.V.M., we do not have any concrete details, but we know the essential: the parishioners were taken to Treblinka with their neighbors probably sometime in August 1942.

Nothing more is to be found about the Christians in the Warsaw ghetto after the great *Aktion*. A proper ending of the sad history of the two Roman Catholic parishes in the Warsaw ghetto is to be found not only in the sympathetic farewell offered by a Jewish friend, but also in the poetic expression of the postwar writer Hanna Krall. In her Polish short story "Salvation" ("Zbawienie") we read: "When the Germans cleared the church of all the Christian Jews, there was only one Jew left in the church: the crucified Jesus. . . . Jesus came down from the cross and called [to the painting] of his mother: 'Mame, kim . . .' This means in Yiddish: 'Come, Mamma.' She [came down and] went to the *Umschlagplatz*" (Krall 1995, 54).[9]

9. Krall, who is not herself religious, cites these lines as one of the numerous, poignant Jewish-Christian anecdotes told in the ghetto.

CHAPTER SEVEN

Concluding Observations

What struck me most in writing the preceding pages was the relative paucity of materials about the Christians in the Warsaw ghetto written by Christians. In comparison to other Jews in the ghetto, few Jewish Christians wrote about their experiences either during the war or, more important, after it. I believe this can in part be explained by their double estrangement in the ghetto: they were removed from their fellow Christians outside the Wall, and they felt rejected by the Jews inside the ghetto; doubtless some themselves shunned the company of Jews. As we have seen (chap. 5, n. 6), some of those who survived were like many survivors of horrible experiences: they tried to forget the past, or at least not to speak or write about it; they wanted to move on with "ordinary" life.

But there is also no doubt in my mind that some of the Christian Jews, especially the neophytes, often felt that they were victims of prejudice coming not only from Jews but also from non-Jews. This latter prejudice is not easy to define. Often an anecdote can be of help in illustrating the complex and contradictory attitudes of the simple anti-Semitic folk toward Jewish converts to Christianity. The following is such a "folkloric" anecdote, jotted down by Adam Czerniaków on January 7, 1940: "Madame Wiktoria [a convert] relates that her neighbor from the burnt house [in September 1939] in Swietokrzyska Street told her that the tenants owed their lives to her prayers alone. The proof is in the fact that only a Jew, Pompinski, a musician, died in the fire with his mother and wife. . . . Madame W. told her acquaintance that she was also Jewish. Yes, was the reply, but you were baptized ten years ago and that saves you" (1999, 106).

135

I realize that Jewish and non-Jewish prejudice against the converts is not new. The rule seems to be that the less spiritually inclined a person is, the more suspicious he or she is of the convert. Such prejudice is embedded in the Polish language. Among Jews, a Jew converted to Christianity is either the quite pejorative Yiddish *mekhes,* or its usual Polish equivalent *wychrzta,* which corresponds to the English "baptized out," suggesting thus "baptized out from among us." Among Christians the term for someone converting from Judaism to Christianity is *przechrzta,* which means something like "baptized over," close to the meaning of English "turncoat."[1] These terms are occasionally interchanged. Thus Jews may use *przechrzta,* but non-Jews would hardly say *wychrzta.* In any case both terms are frankly pejorative: a Jew would not use the term *wychrzta* (or *przechrzta*) about a person whom he respects, and a convinced Christian would not use the term *przechrzta* to describe a new and sincere Christian. These pejorative terms for a convert to Christianity express a negative attitude but also, and more specifically, suggest that the speaker doubts the authenticity or sincerity of the conversion. The persistence of prejudices concerning converts held by non-Jews after the war, and particularly after 1968, goes well beyond the scope of this work.

In the postwar years, official censorship and self-censorship hindered public discussion of many matters concerning Jewish-Polish relations in general and the fate of the ghetto-dwelling Christians in particular (see Anders 2001, 36). Thus forty-five years of censorship, self-censorship, half-truths, "official" truths, lies, and silences have made discussions of a difficult problem in Jewish-Polish relations, that is, conversions, even more difficult. Since the fall of the Communist regime, there have been an increasing number of publications treating these complex matters. While some of the new voices are either unwilling or incapable of relinquishing stereotypical views, or too eager to adopt apologetic or accusatory postures, there have been many publications analyzing the painful past in a spirit of comprehension and empathy for all human suffering. Two excellent examples are the special English-language

---

1. Another philological point: the plural of *przechrzta* and *wychrzta* is most often used in a clearly pejorative form, for it ends in -*y* rather than in -*i.* The -*y* ending refers to things and animals. In the same way, the Polish for Jews *Żydzi* is normal, but *Żydy* is pejorative. (In the singular, the word *Żyd* [*Zhid*] is not pejorative in Polish, despite the contrary belief widely held in America—perhaps because the Russians adopted the Polish *Zhid* as a pejorative term in their language.)

issue of the Polish monthly *Więź* (see *Under One Heaven*, 1998)[2] and Marinowicz's works (1995, 1999).

I believe that the only positive responses to sullen silence and repeated stereotypes are factual studies of historically specific situations and attitudes. And I hope that my own work will be a modest contribution to such studies.

———

The different points of view between Jews and Christian Jews concerning the very nature of conversions is probably the most obvious single conclusion to be drawn from my work. We have seen that Jewish writers from the Warsaw ghetto often expressed dislike, exasperation, bewilderment, or a mixture of all three at the idea of a fellow Jew becoming Christian. These feelings stem, as I discussed in the introduction, from age-old concepts of Jewishness and of apostasy. These reactions were rationalized, particularly by nonreligious writers, by assuming only materialistic, self-seeking reasons for conversion, which in turn supported and justified the dislike and exasperation. We have seen this attitude expressed most systematically by Ringelblum and Małowist. Ringelblum simply does not speak about religious motivations. Małowist, however, contributes something important: he stresses that for many converts the guiding reason for "baptizing out" was an inability or unwillingness to live among the Jews like a Jew. Thus when Małowist talks about people like Dr. Józef Stein, wishing they would return to their Jewishness, he probably does not have in mind that they should return to the prewar Jewish Orthodox milieu; he is simply expressing the hope that they would serve the postwar Jewish community with their talents and that their professional and scientific prestige would profit that community. In other words, Małowist hopes that they would cease to be assimilationists, while remaining assimilated and fully conscious of their Jewishness.

The distinction that Ringelblum, Małowist, and others made between assimilationist and assimilated Jews is difficult to maintain. Notice that the Jewish Christians talk about themselves as being assimilated, whereas Jewish writers reproach them and others for being assimilationists. The term "assimilationist" suggests a person who believes in assimilation and promotes it.

———

2. *Więź* (The Bond) is a Catholic monthly published in Warsaw since 1958. Between 1958 and 1997 it published many articles on various Polish-Jewish subjects. The list of those articles in the special issue of 1998 contains almost 200 items.

The suspicion that the assimilated Jews *promote* the assimilation of others was expressed often by Ringelblum. It is doubtless this suspicion that explains why Ringelblum, Małowist, and others virtually replaced the term "assimilated" with the term "assimilationist."

Ringelblum often speaks about assimilation with almost the same alarm as if he were speaking about conversion. In May 1942, for example, he writes:

> Jonas Turkow acted in Polish repertory this season. The reason: There are no good plays in Yiddish. Besides, this is evidence of the marked assimilation so obvious in the ghetto. The Jews love to speak Polish. There is very little Yiddish heard in the streets. . . . [M]y personal opinion is that what we see in the ghetto today is only a continuation of the powerful linguistic assimilation that began even before the war and has become more noticeable in the ghetto. So long as Warsaw was a mixed society, with Jews and Poles living side by side, one did not notice it so acutely; but now that the streets are completely Jewish, the extent of this calamity [Ringelblum 1988: "this process"] forced itself upon one's attention. (1958, 289; Ringelblum 1988a, 388)

Because he is speaking from a secular viewpoint about the situation in the Warsaw ghetto, Ringelblum places assimilationists and *mekheses* in the same category. The difference between an assimilationist and a *mekhes* seems to him to be merely one of degree. A *mekhes* is an absolute assimilationist.

We should also remind ourselves that antipathy to those who have changed their allegiance is a widespread phenomenon. There is nothing specifically religious in an aversion to those who have left "us" and joined "them," or have abandoned an intellectually respected ideology and have embraced a more "comfortable" one. People always disapprove of a "turncoat." In my social milieu, in American universities, and before the fall of the Soviet Union, I noticed that former Marxists were very often regarded with suspicion, not only by the Marxists, but even by those colleagues who themselves were never attracted to Marxism. I believe that behind this stereotypical aversion lies the conviction that the person who "converts out" from an ideology does it for less than honorable reasons. The real reasons, many people suspect, is to find a more comfortable place for oneself in the ongoing struggle between two camps. But even if there were no suspicion of a crass materialistic motivation, it is possible that one simply does not like those who have either abandoned their "God that failed," or have chosen their intellectual freedom by leaving the rigorous confines of Marxist ideology.

We have seen that Czerniaków, Ringelblum, and others stress the nonreligious reasons for conversions. They delight in pointing over and over again to cynical or apologetic *mekheses* more or less ashamed of their conversion, and they do not take religious needs and religious thinking into account. Ringelblum is an excellent case in point. He was not a religious Jew, as he himself declared. In January 1942, in a fit of despair, he cursed the "the inhumanity of the Jewish upper class" and concluded: "The entire work of the Jewish Council [*Judenrat*] is an evil perpetrated against the poor that cries to the very heaven. If there were a God in the world, he would have long ago flung his thunderbolts and leveled that whole den of wickedness and hypocrisy of those who flay the hide of the poor" (1958, 245). Although Ringelblum obviously understood the importance of Judaism for the national life of the Jews, and even invited a young learned and pious rabbi, Shimon Huberband,[3] to write a report for the Oneg Shabbath archives from a strictly religious point of view, he treated manifestations of religious life with an unmistakably ironic or sarcastic attitude. We see this not only when he speaks about the *mekheses* but also when he writes about Jews.

The following anecdote illustrates the fundamental difficulties involved in communication between the skeptic and the believer. In his single entry for December 12, 13, 14, 1940, a month after the sealing off of the ghetto, Ringelblum reports: "Some *mekheses* were asked why they are attending the church on Sunday wearing their armbands. They answered that they are attending out of habit" (1988a, 215; absent in Ringelblum 1958). "Habit," like "instinct," is a good "anthropological" explanation of a quaint behavior, but it does not take into account the simple fact that the person asked would not be likely to answer by reciting the Creed, or the church commandment about the Sunday observance. The answer of these Christians cannot possibly be taken as a manifestation of nonbelief. It was tantamount to saying (politely) "It's none of your business."

Both Jews and Christians agreed that there had been some conversions or pseudoconversions undergone for other than religious reasons. The Jewish writers only occasionally mention the real, sincere Christians. But Christians such as Hirszfeld and Rev. Czarnecki see the various degrees of religious

---

3. Rabbi Huberband died in Treblinka during the *Aktion*. His work was published in English (Huberband 1987).

involvement clearly and do not assume an apologetic posture about it. What matters to them—and to me—is that there were many Christians in the Warsaw ghetto who were convinced religious persons, who practiced their religion and did not apologize for their faith. The intensive religious life in the two ghetto parishes testifies to this fact.

In the ghetto we see something like an inverse marranism: converts did not have to fake their Christian religion, instead they were discouraged from manifesting it both by religious Jews—which is easy to understand—and by secular or irreligious Jews. The latter antagonism is less understandable to the average Christian, but it is easily grasped by anyone who knows that the concept of Jewishness held by Jews for centuries is diametrically opposed to the concept of religion held by Christians.

There remain a few words to be said about the distinction between the recent and the old converts. There were many Christians in the ghetto who were not converts themselves, but descendants of converts. The Jewish sources imply that the descendants of converts attempted as a rule to hide their origin. This again is a stereotypical judgment. There were many who did not. I found an interesting testimony to that effect. Marian Fuks's short chapter "Christians in the Warsaw Ghetto" ends with the "author's personal digression." I translate:

> The victims of the Holocaust were Jews, but also persons of Jewish origin, including Christians. Many of those victims were so Polonized that they often did not remember or did not know their origin. There is the example of my own family. There was nothing of renegation [*zaprzaństwo*] in [our] attitude. Rather, there was pride in our origins. My family underscored the "Polishness" of its roots. My father was an ardent follower of Piłsudski and his Legions. He bragged about the patriotism of his ancestors, one of whom was wounded [fighting the Russians] in the Jewish troops of Berek Joselewicz [in the Kościuszko uprising of 1793–94]. On my mother's side . . . [here Fuks proudly lists his maternal ancestors, Polish patriots all]. Were they really Jews? [I doubt it] especially given that so many of them, like some of my own relatives, left Judaism and through [inter]marriages disappeared from the Jewish horizon; though only until the time of Hitler. (1999, 67)

Fuks's personal digression applies as well to Janina Landy's family, except that their Polish patriotism was always accompanied by a strong faith in social justice and social progress. Like the Fukses, the Landys kept their name (probably a Gallicized form of Landau). In Poland, generally speaking, changing or retaining a family name was a strong indication of the nature of the conversion. But we must also remember that during the war people in hiding, Jews and non-Jews, assumed false names and avoided Jewish-sounding names. Ringelblum, for example, became Rydzewski. In accidental encounters with prewar Jewish schoolmates or friends hiding on the "Aryan" side, we developed a verbal protocol. Thus, meeting a colleague by the name of Totenberg, I would say, "How are you? I am afraid I have forgotten your name." He would answer: "Tarnowski, of course." But we have seen that many converts retained family names easily recognizable as Jewish, such as Landy, Fuks, Hirszfeld, Lindenfeld, Pfau, Ettinger, and countless others.

But the inverse is not necessarily true. As in America, people change their names for all sorts of reasons other than camouflage. When the famous Dr. Henryk Goldszmit took the pseudonym of Janusz Korczak it was certainly not to hide his Jewishness. Still, assuming a Polish name by a *mekhes* was considered by many, Jews and non-Jews alike, as "proof" of the insincerity of a conversion. This was probably true in the case of Józef Szeryński (previous name: Jósef Andrzej Szynkman), the head of the Order Service in the ghetto. But, on the other hand, we have the case of Marianowicz, who kept his *nom de guerre* but has never hidden his origin.

The main point that I would stress is this: each conversion is different and each conversion would require its own history to be understood. In this domain, stereotyping is simply not productive.

With respect to the baptisms in the ghetto, some Jewish chroniclers or diarists are simply wrong. According to them, these conversions were motivated by a desire to "pass" for "Aryans," or to receive an Italian visa, or some white bread, or more soup or sugar. This opinion does not withstand close examination. We have seen that there could be—indeed, there were—some purely interested conversions at the very beginning of the war. But soon both the Nazi definition of a Jew (December 1, 1939) and, more practically, the rage against the "Jew Kott" (January 20, 1940) would put an end to such purely practical conversions. And contrary to what was thought in the ghetto at large, the priests did not press anyone into baptism. In fact, one normally had to pass a six-week course in the basic tenets of the faith to be baptized.

I think that this particular discrepancy between the Jewish and the Jewish Christian point of view also stems from a misunderstanding. The Nativity of the B.V.M. and All Saints and, until November 15, 1940, Saint Augustine sometimes gave certificates simply testifying that the bearer was a Christian.

Since they were not baptismal certificates, they had little value. More valuable were baptismal certificates made up with the names of deceased baptized persons, or false names on baptismal certificates pretending to originate from a parish in Soviet-occupied Poland. In prewar Poland, as we know, the baptismal certificate of Catholic, Protestant, Uniate, and Greek Orthodox churches stood for the birth certificate. Rabbis also issued de facto birth certificates for Jews. In the first months of the war such certificates were given to everyone who asked, and who could be trusted, because the issuing of such illegal documents was dangerous, indeed would soon be punishable by death. Rev. Czarnecki describes the people who obtained those certificates. They were never considered as converts but simply as people who needed false papers. We must remember that there were many people, Jews and non-Jews alike, who were in hiding from various German repressions, and most of them used false identity papers.

Finally, I must consider the problem of sincerity concerning the many Jewish Christians who participated in the life of the two parishes. People who became Christians in Poland did not belong to the Mosaic confessional milieu. Many of them had left that milieu many years and even many generations before they converted. Many of them became Christians in order to fill religious needs. One fact is obvious to me: in Poland before and during the war, it was almost impossible for an irreligious Jew to return to religious Judaism, since observances were either Orthodox or Hasidic. There was practically no Reformed version of Judaism, like the one in Hungary, Austria, Western Europe, and in America.[4]

As we have already seen, only a very critical, strongly religious person such as Chaim Kaplan states the religious dilemma clearly. In a passage already quoted, speaking about the "apostates among the Jews . . . people educated in a foreign culture," he concludes, "Ossified Judaism did not furnish them with the strength necessary to continue their national lives, and even though they knew in advance that race would still be a handicap for them, it did not prevent them from taking the formal step of leaving Judaism" (1999, 249). Kaplan's words "to continue their national lives" probably stand for

4. The Great Synagogue on Tłomackie Street was built in 1878 by the group of the "progressive" (*postępowi*) Jews in Warsaw, a little on the model of a Jewish German congregation for assimilating upper-class Jews. But the services in the synagogue were Orthodox, although the preaching was in Polish (even though Russian authorities had formally forbidden the use of Polish in synagogues in 1871). For the history of the attempts to create something like Reformed Jewish congregations in Warsaw, culminating in the establishment of the Great Synagogue, see Guterman (1991, 181–211).

"continue to be part of 'national' Judaism, *Knesses Israel*," but for him, as an observing Jew, maintaining one's Jewishness required a support of religious conviction. But many Jews, like the young women described by Hirszfeld, were alienated from religion because for them it represented the Orthodox or Hasidic traditions. In the Warsaw ghetto, especially after November 15, 1940, conversions were answers to a search for faith or a community of faith among those persons who had no sense of belonging to the "national" Judaism. These were most probably genuine spiritual phenomena, even if they were heightened by those wartime horrors which tend, as we know, to make religious people more religious, and irreligious people more irreligious.

———

The history of the Jewish-Christian communities in the Warsaw ghetto is a microhistory. It is a small part of the far larger tragedy of the Warsaw ghetto and of the entire Shoah. This microhistory is a striking testimony to the complexity of the *Zwangsgesellschaft*. Since we are living in a time when the last survivors are passing away, authentic memory has become more difficult to maintain. The Shoah becomes more and more like a mythical entity, and the memory of its true complexity and detail tends to dim.

The history of the Jewish Christians is also a powerful reminder of the larger significance of the Shoah. The presence not just of scattered individuals but of organized Christian parishes in the ghetto illustrates, to my mind better than anything else, the absolutely pseudoscientific, racist character of the Shoah. For the Nazis, Jews were no longer members of religious sociocultural groups but something mysteriously biological. This racist idea, discovered and propagated by several pseudoscientific thinkers in the calamitous nineteenth century, found its medical, social, and political doctrine in the Hitler movement. While such Nazi attitudes are known, of course, to all who remember the Shoah, they must be constantly underscored. In this sense, the fact that the Nazis sent Christians in the ghetto to Treblinka with their neighbors must be remembered. It signifies that after many centuries of various forms of anti-Judaism, or anti-Jewishness, the Nazis finally separated those detestable prejudices from historical, social, and religious elements. In an abstract sense, the Nazis became the first and the *absolute* anti-Semites.

Finally, the history of the two parishes has also, for me, a deep religious significance. This history helped to change the centuries-old Christian attitudes toward Judaism. As Dr. Zaleski-Zamenhof implies, the community of All Saints, the ghetto, and the concentration camp experience of the Christian Jews in Warsaw and elsewhere have undoubtedly played a role in the shaping of those changes. It was inevitable that these new attitudes toward Judaism would be translated into the official theological stance of the Catholic Church. The destruction of Jews together with the Christian Jews removed the last vestiges of the age-old *anti-Judaism* of the Church. On Good Friday, as a part of the Universal Prayer, the deacon used to summon the congregation to pray for the "faithless Jews" ("perfidi Iudei"). Now the deacon says, "Let us pray for the Jewish people, the first to hear the word of God, that they may continue to grow in the love of His name and in faithfulness to His covenant." There is no doubt in my mind that this change is, to a large extent, the result of the common persecution and common death of Jews and their brethren, the Christian Jews. So many of them died together. They should be remembered together—and that is the main reason that I prepared this humble epitaph.

BIBLIOGRAPHY

Adelson, Alan, and Robert Lapides, eds. 1989. *Lodz Ghetto: Inside a Community under Siege*. New York: Viking.

Adler, Stanisław. 1982. *In the Warsaw Ghetto, 1940–1943: An Account of a Witness*. Translated from Polish by Sara (Chmielewska) Philip. Jerusalem: Yad Vashem.

Anders, Jaroslaw. 2001. "The Murder of Memory." Review of Jan T. Gross's, *Neighbors: The Destruction of the Jewish Community in Jedwabne, Poland*. *New Republic*, April 9–16, 36–43.

Bartoszewski, Władysław T. 1993. *Los Żydów Warszawy, 1939–1943* [The Fate of the Warsaw Jews, 1939–1943]. Lublin: Towarzystwo Naukowe Katolickiego Uniwersytetu Lubelskiego.

Bartoszewski, Władysław, and Zofia Lewin, eds. 1969. *Righteous among Nations: How Poles Helped the Jews, 1939–1945*. London: Earlscourt Publications.

Bartoszewski, Władysław T., and Antony Polonsky, eds. 1991. *The Jews of Warsaw: A History*. Oxford: Basil Blackwell, and the Institute for Polish-Jewish Studies.

Bednarczyk, Tadeusz. 1995. *Życie codzienne warszawskiego ghetta: Warszawskie ghetto i ludzie (1939–1945 i dalej)* [Daily life of the Warsaw ghetto: The Warsaw ghetto and its people (1939–1945 and after)]. Warsaw: "Ojczyzna."

Ben-Sasson, Havi. 2003. "Christians in the Ghetto: All Saints' Church, Birth of the Holy Virgin Church, and the Jews of the Warsaw Ghetto." *Yad Vashem Studies* 31:153–73.

Berg, Mary. 1945. *Warsaw Ghetto: A Diary*. Edited by S. L. Shneiderman. New York: L. B. Fisher.

Bryskier, Henryk. 1967–68. "Żydzi pod swastyką, czyli getto warszawskie" [The Jews under the swastika, or the Warsaw ghetto]. *Biuletyn ŻIH* no. 62, 77–99; no. 67, 109–32.

Czarnecki, Antoni. 1981. "Parafia Wszystkich Świętych" [The All Saints parish]. 1973. In *Za co groziła śmierć. Polacy z pomocą Żydom w czasie okupacji* [There was the death sentence for it: The Poles who helped the Jews during the occupation], ed. Władysław Smólski, 206–12. Warsaw: Pax.

Czerniaków, Adam. 1968. *Yamon geto Varsha 6 IX 1939–23 VII 1942*. With a facsimile of the Polish manuscript. Edited by N. Blumental, Arieh Tartakower, N. Neck, and Józef Kermish. Jerusalem: Yad Vashem.

————. 1983. *Adama Czerniakowa dziennik getta warszawskiego 6 IX 1939–23 VII 1942.* Edited by Marian Fuks. Warsaw: Polska Akademia Nauk.

————. 1999. *The Warsaw Diary of Adam Czerniakow: Prelude to Doom.* Edited by Raul Hilberg, Stanislaw Staron, and Josef Kermisz. Translated by Stanislaw Staron and the Staff of Yad Vashem. Jerusalem and Chicago: Ivan R. Dee. (1st ed. 1979.)

Demel, Maciej. 1982. *Aleksander Landy: Życie i dzieło. Lekcja pedagogiki i medycyny przyszłości* [Aleksander Landy: Life and Work: A lesson in pedagogy and in the medicine of the future]. Warsaw: Polska Akademia Nauk.

Dobrzański, Roman. 1995. *Oaza Wszystkich Świętych* [The oasis of All Saints]. Video-cassette of a documentary film made for Polish TV, Warsaw.

Edelman, Marek. 1983. *Mémoires du ghetto de Varsovie: Un dirigeant de l'insurrection raconte.* Preface by Pierre Vidal-Naquet. Translated from Polish with additional texts by Pierre Li and Maryna Ochab. Paris: Edition du Scribe.

————. 1990. *The Ghetto Fights.* Introduction by John Rose. London: Bookmarks. (This is a reprint of a pamphlet prepared by an unnamed translator for the Representation of the General Jewish Workers' Union in Poland "Bund," New York, 1946.)

————. 1993a. "Getto walczy" [The ghetto fights on]. In *Los Żydów Warszawy 1939–1945* [Fate of Warsaw Jews, 1939–1945], ed. Władysław Bartoszewski. Lublin: Towarzystwo Naukowe Katolickiego Uniwersytetu Lubelskiego. (1st ed. 1946.)

————. 1993b. *Das Ghetto kämpft.* Translated from Polish by Ewa and Jerzy Czerwiakowski. Introduction by Ingrid Strobl. Berlin: Harald Kater.

Engelking, Barbara. 1986. *"Czas przestał dla mnie istnieć . . ."—analiza doświadczenia czasu w sytuacji ostatecznej* ["Time has ceased to exist for me . . .": An analysis of the experience of time in the final situation]. Warsaw: Wydawnictwo IFiS.

Engelking, Barbara, and Jacek Leociak. 2001. *Getto warszawskie. Przewodnik po nieistniejącym mieście* [The Warsaw ghetto: The guide to the non-existing city]. Warsaw: Wydawnictwo IFiS.

Ernest, Stefan [pseud.]. 2003. *O Wojnie wielkich Niemec z Żydami Warszawy 1939–1943* [On the war between mighty Germany and the Jews of Warsaw, 1939–1943]. Introduced, edited, and annotated by Marta Młodkowska. Warsaw: Czytelnik and ŻIH.

Friedman, Philip. 1976. *Their Brothers' Keepers: The Christian Heroes and Heroines Who Helped the Oppressed Escape the Nazi Terror.* 1957. Foreword by John A. O'Brien. New York: Holocaust Library.

Fuks, Marian. 1999. *Z dziejów wielkiej katastrofy narodu żydowskiego* [From the history of the great catastrophe of the Jewish people]. Poznań: Sorus.

Gawryś, Cezary. 1998. "The Jewish Children." In *Under One Heaven, Poles and Jews,* a special English-language issue of the monthly *Więź*, 203–18.

Godlewski, Piotr, and Wiesław Krzysztofowicz. 1974. "Społeczeństwo polskie wobec zagłady Żydów" [Polish society in the face of the Shoah]. *Więź*, no. 5, 81–101.

Górny, Jechiel. 1942. "Hurbn Varshe" [Destruction of Warsaw]. In the archives of the ŻIH, Ring I-29, typescript, 48 pp.

Grynberg, Michał, ed. 1988. *Pamiętniki z getta warszawskiego, fragmenty i regesty.* Warsaw: Państwowe Wydawnictwo Naukowe.

———, ed. 2002. *Words to Outlive Us: Voices from the Warsaw Ghetto.* Translated from Polish with an introduction by Philip Boehm. New York: Henry Holt. (Trans. of 1988).

Guterman, Alexander. 1991. "The Origins of the Great Synagogue in Warsaw on Tłomackie Street." In *The Jews of Warsaw: A History,* ed. Władysław T. Bartoszewski and Antony Polonsky. Oxford: Basil Blackwell, and the Institute for Polish-Jewish Studies.

Gutman, Yisrael. 1982. *The Jews of Warsaw, 1939–1943: Ghetto, Underground, Revolt.* Translated from Hebrew by Ina Friedman. Bloomington: Indiana University Press.

Heller, Celia. 1980. *On the Edge of Destruction: Jews of Poland between Two World Wars.* New York: Schocken Books.

Hilberg, Raul. 2001. "Gypsies." In *The Holocaust Encyclopedia,* ed. Walter Laqueur, 271–77. New Haven: Yale University Press.

Hirszfeld, Ludwik. 2000. *Historia jednego życia* [The story of a life]. Warsaw: Czytelnik. (1st ed. 1946; 2nd ed. 1957; rpt. 1967, 1989.)

"Hirszfeld, Ludwik (1884–1954)." 1960–61. In *Polski słownik biograficzny* [Polish biographical dictionary], 9:533–35. Wrocław: Polska Akademia Nauk.

Huberband, Shimon. 1987. *Kiddush Hashem. Jewish Religious Life in Poland during the Holocaust.* Edited by Jeffrey S. Gurrock and Robert S. Hirt. New York: Yeshiva University Press.

Iranek-Osmecki, Kazimierz. 1971. *He Who Saves One Life.* New York: Crown Publishers.

Juszkiewicz, Ryszard, et al., eds. 1993. *Those Who Helped: Polish Rescuers of Jews during the Holocaust.* Part 1. Warsaw: Mako.

Kaplan, Chaim A. 1999. *Scroll of Agony: The Warsaw Diary of Chaim A. Kaplan.* Translated and edited by Abraham I. Katsh. Foreword by Israel Gutman. Bloomington. Indiana University Press. (1st ed. 1965; 2nd ed. 1973.)

Katz, Jacob. 1961. *Exclusiveness and Tolerance: Studies in Jewish-Gentile Relations in Medieval and Modern Times.* Institute of Jewish Studies, University College London. Scripta Judaica 3. Oxford: Oxford University Press. (Rpt. New York: Behrman House.)

Kermish, Joseph. 1953. "Mutilated Versions of Ringelblum's *Notes.*" In *YIVO Annual of Jewish Social Science*, 289–301. New York: Yiddish Scientific Institute.

———. ed. 1986. *To Live with Honor and Die with Honor!* . . . *Selected Documents from the Warsaw Ghetto Underground Archives "O.S." ("Oneg Shabbath").* Edited and annotated by Joseph Kermish. Jerusalem: Yad Vashem.

Krajewski, Stanisław. 1998. "'The Jewish Problem' as a Polish Problem." In *Under One Heaven, Poles and Jews,* a special English-language issue of the monthly *Więź*, 60–81.

Krall, Hanna. 1977. *Shielding the Flame: An Intimate Conversation with Dr. Marek Edelman, the Last Surviving Leader of the Warsaw Ghetto Uprising.* Translated by Joanna Stasinska and Lawrence Weschler. New York: Henry Holt.

———. 1995a. *Existenzbeweise.* Translated by Esther Kinsky. Frankfurt: Neue Kritik.

———. 1995b. "Zbawienie" [Salvation]. In *Dowody na istnienie* [Proofs of the existence], 51–56. Poznań: Wydawnictwo a5.

Kulik, Judith. 2003. "The Attitudes towards Jews in the Christian Polemic Literature in Poland in the 16–18th Centuries." In *Jewish-Polish and Jewish-Russian Contacts,* ed. Wolf Moskovich and Irena Fijałkowska-Janik, 58–78. Vol. 11 of *Slaves and Jews.* Jerusalem: The Hebrew University, Center for Languages and Literatures; Gdańsk: Gdańsk University, Institute for Slavic Philology.

Kulski, Julian. 1972. "Wspomnienia o Czerniakowie" [Recollections of Czerniaków]. *Biuletyn ŻIH*, no. 81, 3–15.

Kurek, Ewa. 1992. *Gdy klasztor znaczył życie. Udział żeńskich zgromadzeń zakonnych w akcji ratowania dzieci żydowskich w okresach 1939–1945* [When the cloister meant life: Participation of the female religious congregation in rescuing Jewish children in 1939–1945]. Cracow: Znak.

———. 1997. *Your Life Is Worth Mine: How Polish Nuns Saved Hundreds of Jewish Children in German-Occupied Poland (1939–1945).* Introduction by Jan Karski. New York: Hippocrene Books. (Trans. of 1992.)

———. 2001. *Dzieci żydowskie w klasztorach* [Jewish children in the convents]. Warsaw: Clio. (Exp. ed. of 1992.)

Laqueur, Walter. 1981. *The Terrible Secret: Suppression of the Truth about Hitler's "Final Solution."* New York: Penguin Books. (1st ed. 1980.)

———, ed. 2001. *The Holocaust Encyclopedia.* New Haven: Yale University Press.

Leociak, Jacek. 1997. *Text wobec Zagłady (O relacjach z getta warszawskiego)* [The text and the Shoah (Accounts from the Warsaw ghetto)]. Wrocław: Leopoldianum.

Lewin, Abraham. 1988. *A Cup of Tears: A Diary of the Warsaw Ghetto.* Edited by Antony Polonsky. Translated by Christopher Hutton. Oxford: Basil Blackwell, and the Institute of Polish-Jewish Studies.

Lewin, Aleksander, ed. 1992. *Janusz Korczak w getcie. Nowe źródła* [Janusz Korczak in the Ghetto: New sources]. Warsaw: Latona.

Madajczyk, Czesław. 1970. *Polityka III Rzeszy w okupowanej Polsce* [The Third Reich policy in occupied Poland]. 2 vols. Warsaw: Państwowe Wydawnictwo Naukowe.

Makower, Henryk. 1987. *Pamiętnik z getta warszawskiego październik 1940–styczeń 1943* [Memoirs from the Warsaw ghetto: October 1940–January 1943]. Edited and supplemented by Noemi Makower. Wrocław and Warsaw: Wydawnictwo Ossolinskich.

Małowist, Marian [Władko, pseud.]. 1986. "Assimilationists and Neophytes at the Time of War-Operations and in the Closed Jewish Quarter," In *To Live with Honor*, ed. Joseph Kermish, 620–34. Jerusalem: Yad Vashem.

Margolis-Edelman, Alina. 2003. Review of Roman Polansky's *The Pianist*. *Zeszyty literackie* 81:143–45.

Marianowicz, Antoni. 1995. *Życie Surowo Wzbronione, (1) Moje wojenne wspomnienia. Rozmowy z Hanną Baltyn. (2) Wspomnienia rodzinne* [The strictly prohibited life. (1) My wartime vicissitudes—conversations with Hanna Baltyn. (2) Family reminiscences]. Warsaw: Czytelnik.

———. 1999. *Polska, Żydzi i cykliści: Dziennik roku przestępnego: 1996* [Poland, Jews and cyclists: A journal of the leap year of 1996]. Warsaw: Iskry.

Matywiecki, Piotr. 1994. *Kamień graniczny* [Boundary stone]. Warsaw: Latona.

Morawska, Klementyna. 1960–61. "Michał Landy (1844–1861)." In *Polski słownik biograficzny* [Polish Biographical Dictionary], 16:477.

Pankiewicz, Roman. 1997. *Historia Kościoła i Parafii Narodzenia Najświętszej Maryi Panny przy Alei Solidarności w Warszawie* [History of the church and parish of the Nativity of the Blessed Virgin Mary on Solidarność avenue]. Warsaw: Wydawnictwo Archdiecezji.

Pankowicz, Andrzej. 1989. "Ronikier, Adam Feliks (1881–1952)." In *Polski słownik biograficzny* [Polish Biographical Dictionary], 32:18–21. Wrocław and Warsaw: Polska Akademia Nauk.

Poland. Ministerstwo Informacji. 1942. The German New Order in Poland. London: published for the Polish Ministry of Information by Hutchinson & Co.

———. Ministerstwo Spraw Zagranicznych. 1942. The Mass Extermination of Jews in German Occupied Poland: Note Addressed to the Governments of United Nations on December 10th, 1942. London, New York: published on behalf of the Polish Ministry of Foreign Affairs by Hutchinson & Co.

Polonsky, Antony. 2001. "Polish Jewry." In *The Holocaust Encyclopedia*, ed. Walter Laqueur, 486–93. New Haven: Yale University Press.

Ringelblum, Emanuel. 1948–58. "Notitsn fun Varshever geto" [Notes from the Warsaw ghetto]. In *Bleter far Geshikhte*. Published in installments in the vols. of 1948, 1951, 1952, and 1958.

———. 1951–55. "Notatki z getta" [Notes from the Warsaw ghetto]. In *Biuletyn ŻIH*. Published in installments in the vols. for 1951, 1952, 1954, and 1955.

————. 1952. *Notitsn fun varshever geto*. [Notes from the Warsaw ghetto]. Warsaw: Yiddish Bukh.

————. 1958. *Notes from the Warsaw Ghetto. The Journal of Emmanuel Ringelblum.* Edited and translated by Jacob Sloan. New York: McGraw-Hill. (Rpt. New York: Stockmen Books, 1974.)

————. 1959. *Chronique du ghetto de Varsovie.* Translated by Léon Poliakov, following the version of Jakob Sloan. Paris: Laffont.

————. 1961. *Togbukh fun varshever geto (1939–1942)* [Journal from the Warsaw ghetto (1939–42)]. Vol. 1 of *Ksovim fun geto* [Writing from the ghetto], edited by Tatiana Berenstein et al. Warsaw: Yiddish Bukh.

————. 1962. *Sepolti a Varsavia. Apunti dal ghetto.* Translated by Carlo Rossi Fontonetti. Milan: Mondarori.

————. 1967. *Ghetto Warschau. Tagebücher aus dem Chaos.* Introduction by Professor Dr. Arieh Tartakower. Jerusalem: Institut Yad Washem; Stuttgart: Seewald. (German trans. of 1988b.)

————. 1982. *Warshawa Ghetto: Hoshu 1940–42 no noto.* Translated by Kaori Oshima and Toshio Iritani. Tokyo: Misuzushobou.

————. 1988a. *Kronika getta warszawskiego, wrzesień 1939–styczeń 1943* [Chronicle of the Warsaw ghetto, September 1939–January 1943]. Edited with an introduction by Artur Eisenbach. Notes by Tatiana Berenstein, Artur Eisenbach, Bernard Marek, and Adam Rutkowski. Translated from Yiddish by Adam Rutkowski. Warsaw: Czytelnik.

————. 1988b. *Stosunki polsko-żydowskie w czasie drugiej wojny światowej. Uwagi i spostrzeżenia* [Polish-Jewish relations during the Second World War. Notes and remarks]. Edited by Artur Eisenbach. Warsaw: Czytelnik.

————. 1992. *Polish-Jewish Relations during the Second World War.* Edited with footnotes by Joseph Kermish and Shmul Krakowski. Translated from Polish by Dafna Allon, Danuta Dabrowska, and Dana Keren. Evanston, Ill.: Northwestern University Press. (Trans. of 1988b.)

Rutkowski, Adam. 1963. "O amerykańskiej, francuskiej i włoskiej edycjach *Kroniki Getta Warszawskiego* Emanuela Ringelbluma" [The American, French, and Italian editions of Emanuel Ringelblum's *journal of the Warsaw ghetto*]. *Biuletyn ŻIH*, no. 45/46, 267–80.

————. 1967. "Sprawa Kotta w środowisku żydowskim w Warszawie (styczeń 1940)" [The Kott Affair and the Warsaw Jews (January 1940)]. *Biuletyn ŻIH*, no. 62, 63–75.

Sakowska, Ruta. 1963. "Łączność pocztowa warszawskiego getta" [The Warsaw ghetto postal services]. *Biuletyn ŻIH*, no. 45/46, 94–109.

————. ed. 1980. *Archivum Ringelbluma. Getto warszawskie, lipiec 1942–styczeń 1943* [The Ringelblum archives: The Warsaw ghetto, July 1942–January 1943]. Warsaw: Państwowe Wydawnictwo Naukowe.

———. 1993. *Ludzie z dzielnicy zamkniętej. Z dziejów Żydów w Warszawie w latach okupacji hitlerowskiej, październik 1939–marzec 1943* [People from the closed district: From the history of the Warsaw Jews in the years of the Nazi occupation, October 1939–March 1943]. 2nd ed. rev. and enl. Warsaw: Państwowe Wydawnictwo Naukowe.

———. ed. 1997. *Archiwum Ringelbluma. Konspiracyjne Archiwum Getta Warszawy,* tom I, Listy o Zagładzie [The Ringelblum archives: Secret archives of the Warsaw ghetto, vol. I, Letters about the Shoah]. Warsaw: Państwowe Wydawnictwo Naukowe.

———. 1999. *Menschen im Ghetto. Die jüdische Bevölkerung im besetzten Warschau 1939–1943.* Translated by Ruth Henning. Osnabrück: Fibre Verlag. (German trans. of 1993.)

———. 2001. "Emanuel Ringelblum and the Underground Archive of the Warsaw Ghetto." In *Scream the Truth at the World: Emanuel Ringelblum and the Hidden Archive of the Warsaw Ghetto,* 1–10. New York and Warsaw: Living Memorial to the Holocaust—Museum of Jewish Heritage and ŻIH.

Schadewaldt, H. 1972. "Hirszfeld, Ludwig." In *Dictionary of Scientific Biography,* 6:432–34. New York: Scribner's.

Seeber, Eva. 1964. *Zwangsarbeiter in der faschistischen Kriegswirtschaft. Die Deportation and Ausbeutung polnischer Bürger unter besonderer Berücksichtigung der Lage der Arbeiter aus dem sogenanten Generalgouvernement (1939–1945).* Berlin: VEB Deutscher Verlag der Wissenschaften.

Seidman, Hillel. 1947. *Tog-bukh fun varshever geto* [The Warsaw ghetto diary]. Buenos Aires: Tsentral-farband fun Polishe Yidn; New York: Federatsye fun Polishe Yidn in Amerike.

Smólski, Władysław, ed. 1981. *Za co groziła śmierć. Polacy z pomocą Żydom w czasie okupacji* [There was the death sentence for it: The Poles who helped the Jews during the occupation]. Warsaw: Pax.

Stefańczyk, Iwona. 1997. "Żydzi Chrześcianie w getcie warszawskim" [Christian Jews in the Warsaw Ghetto]. *Polis,* no. 3, 27–31.

Szpilman, Władysław. 1999. *The Pianist: The Extraordinary Story of One Man's Survival in Warsaw 1939–1945 with Extracts from the Diary of Will Hosenfeld.* Foreword by Andrzej Szpilman. Epilogue by Wolf Biermann. Translated by Anthea Bell. London: Gollancz.

———. 2000. *Pianista: Warszawskie wspomnienia, 1939–1945* [The pianist: Warsaw memoirs, 1939–1945]. Foreword by Andrzej Szpilman. Epilogue by Wolf Biermann. Cracow: Znak.

Tec, Nechama. 1986. *When Light Pierced the Darkness: Christian Rescue of Jews in Nazi-Occupied Poland.* New York: Oxford University Press.

Tomaszewski, Irene, and Tecia Werbowski. 1994. *Zegota: The Rescue of Jews in Wartime Poland.* Montreal: Price-Patterson.

Turkow, Jonas. 1948. *Azoy iz es geven. Hurbn Varshe* [That's how it was: Destruction of Warsaw]. Buenos Aires: Tsentral-farband fun Poylishe Yidn in Argentine.

Under One Heaven, Poles and Jews. 1988. Special English-language issue of the monthly *Więz.* Warsaw.

Władko. See Mołowist, Marian.

Wood, Thomas E., and Stanislaw M. Jankowski. 1994. *Karski: How One Man Tried to Stop the Holocaust.* Foreword by Elie Wiesel. New York: Wiley & Sons.

Wyschogrod, Michael. 1989. *The Body of Faith: God in the People Israel.* New York: Harper & Row.

Zimand, Roman. 1982. *"W nocy od 12 do 5 rano nie spałem." Dziennik Adama Czerniakowa—próba lektury* ["I could not sleep from midnight to 5 in the morning": Diary of Adam Czerniaków—an attempt at a reading]. Warsaw: Państwowy Instytut Wydawniczy.

INDEX

PETER F. DEMBOWSKI

is Distinguished Service Professor (Emeritus) in the Department of Romance Languages and Literatures at the University of Chicago. Born and raised in Warsaw, Poland, Dembowski was involved in the underground activities of the Polish Home Army and participated in the Polish uprising. He was twice a prisoner of the Germans—first at the infamous prison known as Pawiak, where comrades bribed corrupt Gestapo officials to win his freedom, and later at Stalag XB Sandbostel, where he remained until the prison was liberated by the British. Upon liberation, Dembowski joined the Polish Army in the West. For his war service, he was decorated twice with the Polish Cross of Valor and the Silver Service Cross with Swords.